GENDER EQUALITY IN
PRIMARY SCHOOLS

of related interest

How to Transform Your School into an LGBT+ Friendly Place
A Practical Guide for Nursery, Primary and Secondary Teachers
Dr Elly Barnes MBE and Dr Anna Carlile
ISBN 978 1 78592 349 4
eISBN 978 1 78450 684 1

Can I Tell You about Gender Diversity?
A Guide for Friends, Family and Professionals
CJ Atkinson
Illustrated by Olly Pike
ISBN 978 1 78592 105 6
eISBN 978 1 78450 367 3

That's So Gay!
Challenging Homophobic Bullying
Jonathan Charlesworth
ISBN 978 1 84905 461 4
eISBN 978 0 85700 837 4

Counseling Transgender and Non-Binary Youth
The Essential Guide
Irwin Krieger
ISBN 978 1 78592 743 0
eISBN 978 1 78450 482 3

GENDER EQUALITY
in PRIMARY SCHOOLS

A GUIDE FOR TEACHERS

Helen Griffin

Jessica Kingsley *Publishers*
London and Philadelphia

The accompanying PDFs can be downloaded from
www.jkp.com/catalogue/book/9781785923401

First published in 2018
by Jessica Kingsley Publishers
73 Collier Street
London N1 9BE, UK
and
400 Market Street, Suite 400
Philadelphia, PA 19106, USA

www.jkp.com

Library of Congress Cataloging in Publication Data
Names: Griffin, Helen, author.
Title: Gender equality in primary schools : a guide for teachers / Helen
    Griffin.
Description: London ; Philadelphia : Jessica Kingsley Publishers, 2018.
Identifiers: LCCN 2018001694 | ISBN 9781785923401
Subjects: LCSH: Sex differences in education--Great Britain. | Education,
    Primary--Curricula--Great Britain. | Education, Primary--Social
    aspects--Great Britain. | Transgender youth--Education--Great Britain. |
    Educational equalization--Great Britain.
Classification: LCC LC212.93.G7 G75 2018 | DDC 379.2/6--
dc23 LC record available at https://lccn.loc.gov/2018001694

British Library Cataloguing in Publication Data
A CIP catalogue record for this book is available from the British Library

ISBN 978 1 78592 340 1
eISBN 978 1 78450 661 2

Printed and bound by CPI Group (UK) Ltd, Croydon, CR0 4YY

To my brother, Laurence Griffin (1951–2017),
whose love, support and influence will always be with me.

Acknowledgements

First, I would like to thank Heather Hunt and all the teachers, volunteers and children involved in the Gender Respect Project from which this book grew and to the Development Education Centre South Yorkshire (DECSY) for supporting me in this endeavour.

Thanks also to members of my family: Rheanna and Maya Griffin and Laurence Hallam, with whom I had many a lively discussion about gender equality in schools, and to my partner Rob Unwin who was an excellent sounding board for my thinking and gave invaluable feedback on the manuscript.

Thanks are also due to my friends Kate Whittaker, Rosie Carnall and Ruth Chuck who helped me to think about gender issues during our long walks in the countryside and to Alice, Carys, Miranda, Saskia and Caitlin for their interesting reflections about their primary school experiences from their perspectives as young women in their late teens.

Finally, my heartfelt thanks to Laura Church, my volunteer copy-editor, who was so willing to offer her skills to support the writing of this book while working full-time and looking after two young children.

Contents

Preface

This book is based on the Development Education Centre South Yorkshire (DECSY)'s 'Gender Respect Project' (2013–2016). This project grew out of One Billion Rising which inspired women and girls, and men who love them, to come out on the streets of more than 50 different cities across the globe on 14 February 2013. They called for the end of violence to women and girls in a life-affirming demonstration of dance, banners and testimonies. The internet and social media were particularly relevant in this mobilisation and also in capturing the connecting power of seeing women in Kabul, Delhi, Manila, New York and Sheffield out on the streets doing the same dance. One Billion Rising stimulated a debate at Westminster calling for much more attention to relationships education in schools.

The Gender Respect Project aimed to help children and young people to understand, question and challenge gender inequality and violence in a local–global context. It brought together teachers of pupils aged 4–14, creative practitioners and young people to develop engaging, participatory and creative curriculum activities and materials which questioned gender stereotyping (while engaging boys as well as girls), gave global and historical contexts for gender relations and explored issues of power, freedom and human rights in the context of gender. Finally, it was felt essential that children were empowered to take action if they wished to.

PART 1

WHAT IS GENDER EQUALITY EDUCATION AND WHY IS IT IMPORTANT?

Chapter 1

INTRODUCTION

'Originally we thought that sexism wasn't such a big problem but now it's absolutely ginormous. We thought it was just a small thing but now we realise it's global, all over the world.'

(Boy, aged nine)[1]

Primary school-aged children participating in the Gender Respect Project[2] found talking about gender issues remarkably engaging. Being a girl or a boy, even in 21st century Western Europe, is still a hugely important aspect of identity with all sorts of implications for daily life and behaviour, let alone future life chances, physical and mental well being,[3] choices of work[4] and access to money[5] and power.[6] With the global phenomenon of gender-based violence, whether you are male or female can be literally a matter of life or death with, on average, two women being killed by their partner or ex-partner every week in England and Wales (Women's Aid Federation of England 2015). Men are disproportionately involved in violence of all kinds. Violent crime statistics for England and Wales in 2011/12 showed that overall, 62 per cent of violence victims were male, while 80 per cent of offenders were male (ONS 2013). Men are over-represented in the prison population with women making up only just over 4 per cent in UK prisons in 2015.

And yet, in primary schools in the UK in the last 20 years, explicit work on gender equality and stereotyping has largely been the interest of only a few dedicated teachers. Since the advent of the English National Curriculum, national Standard Attainment Tests (SATs)[7] testing, Ofsted and comparison of GCSE results, the main focus of any national work on gender has been concern about boys' attainment, particularly in literacy, being on a par with that of girls. More recently, because of national investigations into incidents of child sexual exploitation and female genital mutilation, the UK government has turned its attention to sexual harassment and violence in schools (House of Commons Women and Equalities Committee 2016). An increase in the number of young transgender people[8] has once more brought gender to the attention of schools, which are being challenged during Ofsted inspections to show policy and practice which promotes transgender inclusion and prevents bullying.[9] In all these cases – boys' lack of attainment in literacy, transphobic bullying, sexual exploitation – it is a particular problem which drives initiatives in schools where groups of children are identified as needing targeted support or interventions, and yet one of the underlying causes of all of these is prevailing cultural gender norms and inequality.

GENDER INEQUALITY AS A ROOT CAUSE OF GENDER-BASED VIOLENCE

The Gender Respect Project, on which this book is based, was inspired by the massive global response to violence against women in the form of One Billion Rising[10] on 14 February 2013. On this day, this campaign, which began in 2012, attracted hundreds of thousands of participants all sharing in a dance which, as V-Day founder and award-winning playwright Eve Ensler described, 'expressed our outrage and joy and our firm global call for a world where women are free and safe and cherished and equal' (One Billion Rising 2017) in 207 countries across the world, broadcast by media outlets globally. This problem of violence against women and girls is being responded to globally by, for example, the UN Commission on the Status of Women (CSW57 2013) and locally in grassroots action around the world.

CSW57 defines violence against women as 'any act of gender-based violence that results in, or is likely to result in, physical, sexual or psychological harm or suffering to women and girls, including threats of such acts, coercion or arbitrary deprivation of liberty, whether occurring in public or in private life' (2013, p.2). Globally, 35 per cent of women have experienced physical/sexual violence by a partner and/or sexual violence by a non-partner in their lifetime (of this by far the majority of violence is from a partner; only 7 per cent of women and girls globally have experienced sexual violence from a non-partner in their lifetime); see GHO 2010.

According to CSW57 the root of gender-based violence is 'the historical and structural inequality in power relations between women and men' and this is 'intrinsically linked with gender stereotypes that underlie and perpetuate such violence as well as other factors that can increase women's and girls' vulnerability to such violence' (CSW57 2013, p.2).

The evidence about the causes of violence offers a hopeful message that change is possible. Gender-based violence is not natural or inevitable because of anything intrinsic about men or women or their relationships. A cross-cultural study of domestic abuse found that nearly a fifth of peasant and small-scale societies were essentially free of family violence (Levinson 1989) and another study found societies free of rape (Sanday 1981). The existence of such cultures proves that male violence against women is not the inevitable result of male biology or sexuality. Kimmel (2008) describes the work of a number of social anthropologists who have concluded that gender inequality is one of the most significant causes of male violence: 'those societies in which rape was relatively rare valued women's autonomy (women continued to own property in their own name after marriage) and valued children (men were involved in child rearing)…the lower the status of women relative to men, the higher the rape rate' (Kimmel 2008, p.325).

Gender inequality is an issue relevant to us all; we all have gender identities and are all involved in relationships of power. 'Schools are themselves sites of normalization' where 'the idea of the "normal" child is constructed' (Paechter 2007, p.61). Within schools, social norms can lead to, reflect or allow gender inequality unless they are revealed and challenged. It could be argued that an essential role of education is to uncover the social norms within society at large which support gender inequality, examine the reasons for them and develop alternatives. Revealing and critiquing those same norms in their operation within the school institution would be an essential part of this process. Bringing critical awareness to something which is taken for granted as normal is a vital first step in a process of societal change.

SOME COMMON ASSUMPTIONS ABOUT GENDER EQUALITY IN PRIMARY SCHOOLS

These may be assumptions that you hold, or that you know others who you would like to influence hold (for example, other staff, governors and parents). For some of these assumptions, arguments and information are offered below, and for others reference is made to the chapter in which the issue is examined in more detail.

Assumption 1: There is no problem – we have gender equality in the UK now, don't we?

There are many worrying statistics to choose from which reveal that this is by no means the case, for example, the fact that the UK is slipping down the league table on gender equality internationally. In 2006, Britain was 9th in the World Economic Forum's (2017) gender equality league table, but although there had been some progress from 2016 to 2017, it had moved down overall nine places to 15th in 2017. The UK is 53rd out of 144 countries on economic participation, with the gap mainly due to an imbalance of work between men and women as 57 per cent of the work women do is unpaid compared to 32 per cent of the work men do. The UK is ranked 95th overall for estimated earned income with women's earnings being 66 per cent of men's. The UK is 38th on women in parliament with not only other European countries ahead of the UK on this but also many others in South America and Africa (for example, Bolivia and Rwanda; see World Economic Forum 2017). For statistics relating to sexual harassment and violence in the UK see Chapter 4.

Assumption 2: Although a school might care about gender equality there is little UK government support through Ofsted, for example, for giving time to it.

National legislation and guidance

The main legislative framework that relates to gender equality in the UK is the Equality Act 2010.

> Under the Equality Act 2010, maintained schools and academies, including free schools, must have due regard to the public sector equality duty (PSED). This means that they must take active steps to

identify and address issues of discrimination where there is evidence of prejudice, harassment or victimisation, lack of understanding, disadvantage, or lack of participation for individuals with protected characteristics (these being disability, gender reassignment, pregnancy and maternity, race, religion or belief, sex and sexual orientation). (Equality and Human Rights Commission 2016)

The 2017 Ofsted inspection handbook reflects this duty and states clearly that records and analysis need to be provided of any 'bullying, discriminatory and prejudicial behaviour, either directly or indirectly' in relation to 'racist, sexist, disability and homophobic bullying, use of derogatory language and racist incidents' (p.17) ('sexist' was added in 2016). Leaders and governors are assessed on how well they:

promote all forms of equality and foster greater understanding of and respect of all faiths (and those of no faith), races, genders, ages, disability and sexual orientations (and other groups with protected characteristics),[11] through their words, actions and influence within the school and more widely in the community. (Ofsted 2017, point 39, p.17)

A school will be deemed inadequate if 'Leaders and governors, through their words, actions or influence, directly and/or indirectly, undermine or fail to promote equality of opportunity. They do not prevent discriminatory behaviour and prejudiced actions and views' (Ofsted 2017, p.45). The UK government, in its 'Violence against Women and Girls (VAWG) Strategy 2016–2020', aims to achieve:

a significant reduction in the number of VAWG victims, achieved by challenging the deep-rooted social norms, attitudes and behaviours that discriminate against and limit women and girls, and by educating, informing and challenging young people about healthy relationships, abuse and consent. (HM Government 2016, p.14)

This further indicates a recognition of the importance of gender equality in schools at government level.

Following many years of campaigning by educational organisations and recommendations from various government working groups, including the House of Commons Women and Equalities Committee (2016) which stated, 'By the time they reach secondary school children often have entrenched views about gender norms. It is therefore important that children are educated about gender equality, consent, relationships and sex in an age-appropriate way starting in primary school', in 2017 the UK Government proposed 'the (mandatory) introduction of the new subject of "relationships education" in primary school and renaming the secondary school subject SRE as "relationships and sex education", to emphasize the central importance of healthy relationships' (DfE 2017). This should be in place by September 2019 and will be an extremely significant justification for primary schools to focus on developing respectful relationships across all genders and sexualities.

International agreements
UNITED NATIONS (UN) CONVENTION ON THE RIGHTS OF THE CHILD
The UK Government ratified the UN Convention on the Rights of the Child in 1991, along with all but two UN member states. Article 2 clearly lays out that all children (under 18) are entitled to have their rights met 'without discrimination of any kind, irrespective of the child's or his or her parent's or legal guardian's race, colour, sex, language, religion, political or other opinion, national, ethnic or social origin, property, disability, birth or other status' (OHCHR 1996–2017). Other articles which relate to gender equality are Article 19 on protection from violence, Article 34 which states that parties must take any steps necessary to protect children from all forms of sexual exploitation and abuse and Article 39 which states that parties must take the appropriate measures to promote the recovery of a child from any form of neglect, abuse or maltreatment.

SUSTAINABLE DEVELOPMENT GOALS
Each of the 193 UN member states adopted a global development framework in September 2015 at the summit in New York, known as the Sustainable Development (or Global) Goals (SDGs). These:

> commit all signatory countries to tackle issues as diverse and deep-rooted as gender inequality, climate change, access to quality education and the promotion of peaceful and inclusive societies. The SDGs officially came into force on 1 January 2016 and the UK must now move forward with implementing the goals at home and supporting other countries to achieve them overseas. (House of Commons International Development Committee 2016, p.6)

The goals most relevant to gender equality and education and which have to be implemented domestically by the UK government are goals 4: 'Ensure inclusive and equitable quality education and promote lifelong learning opportunities for all', 5: 'Achieve gender equality and empower all women and girls' and 10: 'Reduce inequality within and among countries'.[12]

Assumption 3: Gender differences are natural/innate and to do with brain differences and hormones, etc. – boys are naturally more physical and boisterous than girls, etc.

This is an argument, seen as 'common sense', that is pervasive in education and wider society and one that it is essential to address as it may underlie a teacher's hesitation to fully engage in gender equality work in primary schools. This assumption is largely addressed in Chapter 2 of this book.

Assumption 4: Children learn their gender identities through socialisation.

Teachers who are aware that biology has very little power in explaining gender differences may revert to simple socialisation theories which are also inadequate accounts of the development of gender identities. More complex explanations of the social construction of gender have developed over the last 30 years. This is explained in Chapter 2.

Assumption 5: Even if gender identity is learnt then societal influences (media, family, peer group) are too powerful for schools to be able to make any difference.

There is a growing body of school-based research evidence of what works in schools to challenge stereotypes and social norms. The second part of this book is based on good practice in primary schools, that is, work that has been shown to be effective in challenging stereotypes, widening choices and improving gender relationships.

Assumption 6: We should be focusing on raising boys' achievement in literacy.

It is a fact that there is still a significant (6%) gap between boys and girls' attainment in literacy at Key Stage 2 (KS2) SATs (Moss and Washbrook 2016). Understandably, schools are concerned about this gap and want to narrow it. Unfortunately many schools base their practices on a plethora of advice which puts the emphasis on 'boy-friendly' books and teaching methodologies. This is in spite of a wealth of well-researched counter-evidence (for example, Moss and Washbrook 2016) which rigorously challenges such approaches as being ineffective for any pupils regardless of gender because of the way they reinforce gender stereotypes. 'One of the reasons why there have been such disappointing results for schools which have adopted some of the strategies to raise boys' achievement is that they have encouraged teachers and pupils to view boys and girls as gender stereotypes' (Skelton, Francis and Valkanova 2007, p.61).

Rather than reinforcing stereotypes by providing a 'boy-friendly' literacy curriculum it is important to address the multiple factors which lead to the reading gender gap (and any other gender gaps which might affect girls adversely). Gender-based teacher expectations, for example, have been shown to have a significant impact on pupil performance.

Gender differences in student attitudes towards learning have also been shown to be detrimental to both girls and boys and have led to guidance such as this, from the Institute of Physics' in-depth study of gender in secondary schools: 'Specifically, schools should ensure that girls develop their self-confidence and resilience – they must not be afraid to fail sometimes – and boys should be persuaded of the link between hard work and high levels of achievement' (Institute of Physics 2015, p.16).

Much of the literature points to the importance of providing excellent quality teaching and learning opportunities in schools for all pupils.

> Research has shown that encouraging children to work together on carefully designed, open-ended tasks can enhance the quality of thinking and engagement… [It recommends using] whole class teaching to model giving others time to think and tentatively explore particular issues; asking open questions; expecting and encouraging

extended talk rather than one word answers. Use this as a basis to introduce dialogic talk. (DCSF 2009, p.13)

The answer is to avoid stereotyping children's identities and for educators to take an active role in planning for, supporting and developing individual children's identities as masterful learners of a broad and balanced curriculum. (Siraj-Blatchford and Clarke 2000, quoted in Moss and Washbrook 2016, p.49)

Assumption 7: It's just about girls, so of no interest to boys.

In the Gender Respect Project the boys were as interested as the girls in discussing stereotyping, as they recognised how it restricted their choices as well as girls. Several of the boys regretted the fact that, at home, they weren't allowed to get involved in knitting, baking or sewing and experienced gendered expectations from relatives on such things as showing feelings:

'My oldest cousin he always called me like girl names – we went to Pleasure Island one day and he told me to ride some right scary rides. I didn't moan [on the rides] so he started calling me [my own name] rather than girls' names.' (Boy, aged nine)

At school, many of the boys saw unfairness in the way they were regarded by teachers, for example, being expected to be disruptive and not believed as much as girls. The boys involved in the Gender Respect Project became as equally fired up to take action to change things in their schools as the girls:

'We extremely disapprove of stereotypes such as tomboys, Ella girls, pink's for girls, football's for boys.' (Boys, aged ten)

This interest from boys for engaging with the topic has been confirmed by other organisations,

David Brockway, who delivers workshops to boys and young men through the Great Men project, told the House of Commons Women and Equalities Committee that boys wanted the opportunity to engage with Sex and Relationships Education (SRE) and Personal, Social, Health and Economic (PSHE) education but were not always given the chance to do so. 'One school I went to last year…said that for the last six years they have been working with their girls on combating sexual harassment and on body positivity. I said, "What have you been doing with the boys?" and they said, "Nothing; they just watch a video"' (quoted in House of Commons Women and Equalities Committee 2016, p.40).

Not only is gender stereotyping and relationships of interest to boys but it is also recognised generally that engaging boys with these areas is essential for gender equality. As the UK Government's Women and Equalities Committee's report on sexual harassment and sexual violence in schools says, 'too often, SRE ignores the position of boys and young men. It must be broadened to challenge harmful notions of masculinity and reflect boys' experiences. It should also support boys to challenge and reduce sexual harassment and sexual violence' (House of Commons Women and Equalities Committee 2016, p.41).

The idea of 'hegemonic (dominant) masculinity', developed by Connell (1995), has greatly influenced theory on masculinities. Kenway and Fitzclarence (1997, p.207) describe this theory, which recognises that, although there are many masculinities, 'these can be clustered on the basis of general social, cultural and institutional patterns of power and meaning and are built in relationship to each other'. Connell calls these masculinities 'hegemonic, subordinate, complicitous and marginal' (Connell 1995, in Kenway and Fitzclarence 1997, p.207).

'Hegemonic masculinity' is that 'dominant and dominating forms of masculinity which claim the highest status and exercise the greatest influence and authority' (Kenway and Fitzclarence 1997, p.207). For example, this could be White, middle-class, able-bodied and straight men. 'Subordinate masculinity stands in direct opposition to hegemonic masculinity and is both repressed and oppressed by it' (Kenway and Fitzclarence 1997, p.207). This includes gay masculinities and 'any major attachment to the "feminine" is likely to propel its owner into this category and subject him to various forms of violence' (Kenway and Fitzclarence 1997, p.207). Hegemonic masculinity is an ideal of what it means to be a 'real man' that few, if any, actual men can live up to. Nevertheless, whether a man tries to live up to this, or even does not try, he will still benefit from a 'patriarchal dividend...the advantage men in general gain from the overall subordination of women' (Connell 1995, p.79). 'Complicitous masculinities' includes men who may not fit into all the characteristics of hegemonic masculinities but don't challenge them and may aspire to them. They will receive some of the benefits of hegemonic masculinity. The idea of 'marginal masculinities' is where there is interplay of gender with structures such as class and race so, for example, these could be Black, working-class men. These marginal masculinities may 'not be marginal within their own patch' but will only 'wield structural power to the extent that they are *authorised* by the dominant race/class' (Kenway and Fitzclarence 1997, p.208). Femininities which unwittingly support hegemonic masculinity are those which involve 'compliance and service, subservience and self-sacrifice and constant accommodating to the needs and desires of males' (Kenway and Fitzclarence 1997, p.208).

Hegemonic masculinity in Western society:

> mobilises around physical strength, adventurousness, emotional neutrality, certainty, control, assertiveness, self-reliance, individuality, competitiveness, instrumental skills, public knowledge, discipline, reason, objectivity, and rationality... [and distances itself from] physical weakness, expressive skills, private knowledge, creativity, emotional dependency, subjectivity, irrationality, cooperation and empathetic compassionate, nurturant and certain affiliative behaviours. (Kenway and Fitzclarence 1997, p.208)

Violent males 'draw selectively' from hegemonic masculinity, exaggerating, distorting and glorifying the values, attributes and behaviours (Kenway and Fitzclarence 1997). Connell (1995) describes violent males as the 'shock-troops', doing the dirty work of patriarchy. This framing of the issue calls for work in education on challenging and questioning accepted ideas of masculinity. However, this is perhaps one of the more problematic areas of work on gender. Many studies show how parents and carers take care to ensure that their pre-school sons have full acceptance as a boy whereas there is much more acceptance of flexibility for girls, even if this requires a labelling of 'tomboy'. This is likely to be partly related to an unconscious recognition that boys benefit from the 'patriarchal dividend'; there is much more to be gained from being seen as a boy than as a girl in an unequal society. Also parents and carers can fear that boys who do not conform will be subject to teasing and bullying.

There are now many campaigns and organisations globally which specifically look at masculinities. The co-founder of A Call to Men, Tony Porter, shares a powerful message about manhood and the role of men in preventing domestic and sexual violence in his TEDWomen talk (TEDWomen 2010). He asks men everywhere not to 'act like a man' and by telling powerful stories from his own life, he shows how this mentality, drummed into so many men and boys, can lead men to disrespect, mistreat and abuse women and each other. His solution is to break free of what he calls the 'man box'.

Assumption 8: Gender equality is not an issue in primary schools – if we bring attention to it, it will create a problem which wasn't there before.

I hope that this whole book challenges this notion. Associated arguments might be 'we treat them all the same' or 'they're too young to understand' and 'children shouldn't have to worry about such things' which fits into a common notion of childhood innocence. Chapter 2 provides an explanation of the development of gender identities from a young age and therefore the importance of catching children before stereotypes become entrenched. Chapters 3 and 4 illustrate how primary school-aged children have formulated ideas about gender roles, relationships, gendered expectations and fairness, whether we engage with them in schools or not. It is hoped that bringing children's critical attention to gender equality will contribute to the solution of a problem that is definitely there for them in primary schools and later in adolescence and adult life. The second part of the book focuses on ways of positively engaging primary school-aged children on these issues.

Assumption 9: It's just about PSHE and SRE.

Explicit teaching about gender equality may well find its place in the PSHE and SRE curriculum in primary schools (DfE 2017), but it is essential for gender equality to be part of a whole-school approach. Examples of what schools can do in other curriculum areas can be found in Chapter 6.

Assumption 10: Creating a gender equal environment and providing positive role models is enough.

Although this is necessary, research shows that this is not sufficient to change ideas and attitudes towards gender. The evidence points towards the importance of discussion, critical awareness and addressing issues directly. Teachers in the Gender Respect Project were all trained in Philosophy for Children (P4C) methodology and so used P4C to develop children's critical thinking about gender issues. Chapter 7 includes ideas for how to use P4C to think about gender issues as well as other examples of how to engage children in explicit discussion about gender.

In Part 2 of this book the practical ideas for implementing gender equality follow a model which has been given the acronym 'ICE': Implicit, Curriculum, Explicit. 'Implicit' includes everything in a school that gives out messages about gender: displays and materials, language use, gendered expectations, ethos and relationships and the 'hidden' curriculum. 'Curriculum' includes ensuring that the 'taught curriculum' is gender-inclusive, for example: who is studied in history; what examples are used in maths; how genders are portrayed in English and so on. 'Explicit' is how gender issues can be explicitly discussed and critical awareness developed.

Assumption 11: Work on addressing gender equality *per se* is not relevant to meeting the needs of transgender pupils, which should be our main priority.

Creating a whole-school environment where gender stereotyping is eliminated or challenged, if it does occur, allows all children to flourish and develop their individual identities without having to conform to perceived gender norms. As is explained further in Chapter 2, the way children manifest their gender identities is constrained by wider society, parents and the media forming a 'marketplace' of gender options, which is then policed by peers. Research has shown that gender non-conforming children, unless they are in positions as confident leaders in their peer groups, experience bullying.

> The literature indicates that…children instruct peers about the content of cultural gender stereotypes; exclude peers on the basis of gender; tease peers concerning violations of gender norms; and in extreme cases, harass and physically attack peers who are gender atypical. (Lamb *et al.* 2009, p.361)

Over the last few years primary schools have needed to respond to the rise in the number of children identifying as transgender or non-binary. The guidance from organisations working on transgender issues in schools points to the need to be proactive rather than just reacting to perceived problems that individual children may present. This means that schools need to work on gender diversity, helping children to behave, have interests and present themselves in ways that are physically unconstrained by gender labels. Not only will this ensure that individual children's choices are widened but that those children whose felt gender identity doesn't conform to the stereotypes of the sex they were assigned at birth will feel accepted and 'normal'. Evidence shows that there is a particularly strong connection between the perception of masculine identities and sexuality. Research has identified the ways in which many parents are concerned to ensure gender conformity with their sons to avoid them being perceived as too feminine and therefore prone to being bullied by their peers, and encourage their heterosexuality.

> Parents of sons reported negative responses to their sons wearing pink or frilly clothing; wearing skirts, dresses, or tights; and playing dress up in any kind of feminine attire. Nail polish elicited concern from a number of parents too, as they reported young sons wanting to have their fingernails or toenails polished. Dance, especially ballet, and Barbie dolls were also among the traditionally female activities often noted negatively by parents of sons. (Kane 2006, p.160)

> A white, upper-middle-class, heterosexual father concerned about public crying, said about his five-year-old son 'I don't want him to be a sissy...I want to see him strong, proud, not crying like a sissy.' (Kane 2006, p.161)

In spite of recent changes in society towards acceptance of lesbian, gay and bisexual identities there is still a tendency for boys and men to distance themselves from femininity for fear that this will cause others to challenge their heterosexuality. 'Passivity and excessive emotionality, as well as more material adornments of femininity, are precisely what must be avoided in this hegemonic version of masculinity' (Kane 2006, p.153). 'Heterosexual performances are integral to the production of a "real boy"' (Renold 2007, p.279). It is sometimes seen to be okay to be a gay man if you are a gay man but not okay for there to be any doubt or confusion about your sexuality if you are a straight man.

So gender equality issues are inextricably connected to LGBT+[13] (lesbian, gay, bisexual, transgender) equality issues from the point of view of creating a school climate and curriculum that celebrates gender diversity. Homophobic, transphobic and sexist bullying can be tackled effectively only by schools where there is a willingness to engage fully with implementing gender equality.

Assumption 12: You shouldn't talk about boys and girls any more as this is too gender binary; gender is fluid and non-binary and language needs to include all genders.

It is true that teachers referring to girls and boys incidentally everyday (and still some even lining them up boy, girl, boy, girl) unnecessarily emphasises gender binaries. However, while there are still obvious differences between girls and boys' experiences and how they 'do' their gender and unequal power differences that can only be talked about with reference to 'girls', 'women', 'boys' and 'men', these labels are still relevant. Once we have an entirely gender equal society then we can do away with defining any gender difference (or expand the language to reflect the many gender identities that a person could identify with – which seems to be happening in relation to LGBT+ currently). I have referred to 'girls' and 'boys' in this book, where necessary, without implying fixed, binary gender categories.

A NOTE ON DEFINITIONS

Language is constantly in a process of change but at the time of this book these are the relevant definitions (Safe Zone Project n.d.):

Biological Sex (noun) – A medical term used to refer to the chromosomal, hormonal and anatomical characteristics that are used to classify an individual as female or male or intersex. Often referred to as simply 'sex', 'physical sex', 'anatomical sex', or specifically as 'sex assigned [or designated] at birth'.

Gender Expression (noun) – The external display of one's gender, through a combination of dress, demeanor, social behaviour, and other factors, generally measured on scales of masculinity and femininity. Also referred to as 'gender presentation'.

Gender Fluid (adj.) – Gender fluid is a gender identity best described as a dynamic mix of boy and girl. A person who is gender fluid may always feel like a mix of the two traditional genders, but may feel more man some days, and more woman other days.

Gender Identity (noun) – The internal perception of someone's gender, and how they label themselves, based on how much they align or don't align with what they understand their options for gender to be. Common identity labels include girl, boy, man, woman, genderqueer, trans and more.

Heteronormativity (noun) – The assumption, in individuals or in institutions, that everyone is heterosexual, and that heterosexuality is superior to all other sexualities. Leads to invisibility and stigmatising of other sexualities. Often included in this concept is a level of gender normativity and gender roles, the assumption that individuals *should* identify as men and women, and be masculine men and feminine women, and finally that men and women are a complimentary pair.

LGBT+ – Lesbian, gay, bisexual, transgender.

Non-binary (adj.) – Any gender that is not exclusively male or female.

Trans/Transgender (adj.) – (1) An umbrella term covering a range of identities that transgress socially defined gender norms. (2) A person who lives as a member of a gender other than that expected based on anatomical sex.

HOW THIS BOOK IS ORGANISED

The first part of this book (Chapters 2 to 4) gives some theoretical and research background to gender equality and the second part (Chapters 5 to 7) some practical ideas for implementing gender equality in primary schools. There is a summary of recommendations and possible ways forward in Chapter 8. A summary of key points is provided at the end of each chapter to enable the reader to decide whether to delve into the chapter further. The appendices provide a summary of the scoping study photographs and questions, a checklist for auditing a primary school, a checklist for evaluating children's books and a list of recommended children's books. The chapter Notes and References section provide comprehensive references and a Further Reading list is also provided.

SUMMARY

This chapter has:

- introduced why it is important to focus on gender equality education in primary schools

- explained how gender inequality relates to gender-based violence

- examined some common assumptions about gender equality education

- outlined relevant international agreements and national legislation and guidance

- explored why this work is relevant to boys as well as girls

- introduced the rest of the book.

Chapter 2

HOW CHILDREN LEARN TO EXPRESS GENDER

THEORIES ABOUT GENDER IDENTITY DEVELOPMENT

'Most boys are normally, people think they're quite naughty, so I think people would expect me to be good.'

(Girl, aged seven)

One of the key obstacles to gender equality work in schools is a persistent, common-sense belief that girls and boys are innately different from each other. Even people who acknowledge the influence of the environment on children still hold a niggling doubt and this is often based on evidence before their very eyes. It's very difficult to ignore the very compelling, anecdotal evidence of your own young children or children in your classroom. I have been witness to many conversations where other parents have mentioned in passing how boys are more boisterous than girls, for example. I recently overheard two mothers of teenage boys talking about how you have to 'run them' like dogs. Parents have told me about their young boys' fascination in everything with wheels, which seemed to have arisen in spite of trying to interest them in other things, like dolls. Teachers in nurseries talk about how boys like to charge around pretending to be superheroes and need outdoor play to let off steam. The usually unspoken assumption is that these behaviours illustrate an innate difference between girls and boys. It seems that people rarely question this assumption and wonder if there are other factors in play. A close friend of mine told me that when she noticed differences between her son and daughter, which seemed gender stereotypical (such as the son being less talkative, less emotional, more physical), she always questioned her own assumptions, as I had two daughters of similar ages who also showed similar differences even though they were both girls. Lived experience will always seem more compelling than research evidence, as it is more personally significant and therefore powerful. In the concluding article of the *National Geographic* magazine of January 2017, which was devoted to the 'Gender Revolution', Slaughter (2017) quotes Chip Brown who said: 'Some behaviors really do seem innate. My elder son was fascinated with wheels, trucks and construction machinery before he could talk.' There is now a large body of research evidence identifying unconscious parental expectations and reactions as being an important factor in the development of these gendered interests and traits in children. For example, in the study showing how, when mothers were asked to predict whether their 11-month-old baby could crawl up a slope, there were gendered differences in expectations, even though there were no actual differences in the infants' performances (Mondschein, Adolph and Tamis-LeMonda 2000). And even where parents are very consciously trying to raise their young children in a gender-neutral way, environmental factors including the expectations of other people come strongly into play. This is nicely illustrated in the series of Twitter comments and blogs from @GenderDiary published as *The Gender Agenda* (Ball and Millar 2017), where a mother and father produce compelling anecdotal evidence about how their boy and girl child are treated differently and their masculinities and femininities are constructed by society.

For teachers, too, making sense of their own lived experiences of the differences between girls and boys often entails an unexamined belief that these differences must be innate. The logic goes that if they are innate then they are natural and so perhaps good and so we can't or even shouldn't do anything about them. Very often there is little consideration by teachers of the impact of their own perceptions of what boys and girls are like on how children act in the primary classroom, for example, the documented perception that girls achieve through hard work and boys are innately clever. Skelton and Francis (2003) quote Renold's (2001) study where:

> girls were not seen as talented by their teachers but as 'bossy', 'overconfident' and one of them as 'not as clever as she thinks she is'. And teachers in Maynard's (2002) research of a primary school saw underachieving boys as 'having innate if untapped potential'. (p.8)

In the Gender Respect Project's scoping study, when asked if they perceived any unfairness in the way girls and boys were treated in school, several of the children identified teachers as having an expectation that the boys would be naughty and the girls sensible. In 2016, a young man I know who was in his first year of primary teaching in a Year 6 (10–11 years old) class was concerned that girls volunteered to tidy up and be 'teacher's help' every day. After discussing this with me, he specifically decided to ask boys to do it and now he has two enthusiastic boys who often help out, leaving the girls to run around in the playground.

It is essential for teachers to have considered theories of how gender differences arise if they are to become aware of their own unconscious bias, which may have the effect of reinforcing the differences. In the rest of this chapter I give straightforward arguments to refute the idea that gender differences in humans and certain other mammals are innate, and summarise some of the research on how children actually learn to 'do' their gender.

NEUROSCIENCE AND GENDER

In the current UK context popular books such as *Why Mars and Venus Collide* (Gray 2008), *The Female Brain* (Brizendine 2007) and *Why Can't a Woman Be More Like a Man?* (Wolpert 2014) make claims, based on neuroscience, that biologically 'hard-wired' differences between men and women are the cause of differences in behaviour, aptitude and the mind in general. These studies have been used as a basis for so-called 'brain-based learning' and educational initiatives such as separate sex teaching (teaching boys and girls in different ways entirely based on neuroscience rather than for other reasons, such as girls performing better when in single sex groups). As Fine (2010) writes in her book *Delusions of Gender,* a systematic and well argued review of a huge body of evidence which challenges this idea of 'hard wiring':

> neurosexism reflects and reinforces cultural beliefs about gender – and it may do so in a particularly powerful way…dubious 'brain facts' about the sexes become part of the cultural lore…refreshed and invigorated by neurosexism, the gender cycle is ready to sweep up into the next generation. (p.xxviii)

Fine gives an example of where, even in animals, biological differences between males and females have no impact on, for example, parenting roles. Different troops of the same species of macaque monkey in different parts of a continent show different levels of paternal care. In Gibraltar male baby-sitting is so important that 'young females are kept away from infants so that young males may learn their role'. In the very same species in Morocco male care is much less significant, 'while hormones are the same throughout these different species there is no "universal pattern" to how different tasks of society including infant care are divided' (Fine 2010, p.127). Fine points out that, in fact, evidence from neuroscience points towards 'neuroplasticity': not only can we not use neurological differences as proof of essential gender differences, but the neurological differences can be seen to be *caused* by environmental factors. Our brains adapt to our circumstances.

This environmental effect can even be seen with hormones, as Fine details in her subsequent, equally scholarly yet amusing book, *Testosterone Rex* (Fine 2017). Even male rats who normally leave the parenting to the females, when left with a brood of baby rats in a cage will, before too long 'begin "mothering"' them 'in much the same way that females do' (Fine 2017, p.187). Fine refers to an interesting study on testosterone carried out by van Anders with humans (Fine 2017, p.145), where three different groups of men were randomly assigned to care for an artificial baby that could be programmed to respond in different ways. The first group, defined as 'traditional man who lets the woman do the baby care', was instructed to sit and listen to the baby cry. The second group, 'traditional man who lets the woman do the baby care and is therefore woefully inexperienced in that demanding acquired skill but on this occasion has been left alone with a baby', was instructed to interact with the baby but the baby is programmed to cry persistently, regardless of anything they try. The final group was assigned to the group 'progressive dads', with the baby programmed to be consolable. In the first two groups the men's testosterone levels rose whereas in the last group the levels dropped 'as their tender ministrations took their desired effect'. In other words, the crying baby affected testosterone differently depending on the person's ability to deal with the situation.

SOCIAL CONSTRUCTION OF GENDER – SO HOW DO CHILDREN LEARN TO 'DO' GENDER?

In the past, socialisation theories described how children develop their gender identities from the messages given by significant others and by observing how people around them behave (perhaps a bit like the macaque monkeys). When primary-school teachers are asked, as they were at the Gender Respect Project conference and other workshops, this still seems to be a common understanding. However, problems have been identified with these theories, as they made assumptions that identity was fixed and coherent; they failed to account for diversity amongst children who accept some ideas and reject others and, crucially, they ignored any issues of power. Post-structuralist theory, in which the relationship between the individual and social institutions; is seen as inseparable and interdependent, offers the explanation that children don't just soak up their identity from people and institutions; they 'reshape and develop individual identities as they engage with the diverse and often contradictory messages they receive from caregivers, at home, from the media and in preschool settings' (Martin 2011, p.xvi). MacNaughton explains this further:

> The child actively constructs meaning through 'reading' and inter-preting experiences, but is not free to construct any meanings or identities she/he wants. [They are] limited to alternatives made available to them. Children do not enter a 'free marketplace' of ideas but form identities in a highly controlled marketplace. Some meanings are more powerful than others because they are more available, more desirable, more pleasurable and more able to be recognized by others. (MacNaughton 2000, p.24)

The child's carers, peers and teachers will contribute to this 'market-place of ideas' and perhaps present ideas which are alternative to mainstream culture, but mass media, including marketing, will also be sending powerful messages of what it means to be a girl or a boy. Concern about the narrowing of these messages has resulted in such campaigns as 'Let Toys Be Toys'[1] and 'Pink Stinks'[2] where there has been some success in persuading shops to discontinue separating boys and girls' toys into different, clearly labelled areas. Photographs taken for the Gender Respect Project in Sheffield stores in June 2013 show a worrying division between types of toys, with nurturing play featuring for girls and construction or battle play for boys.

Martin (2011), in her two-year longitudinal study of children learning gender in the Early Years, exemplified in detail the processes taking place in a nursery setting (part of a primary school in London) where there was no intervention by staff to challenge gender norms and behaviour, or to support children in expanding these, as they believed that 'girls and boys are innately different' and were basing their teaching on 'developmentally appropriate practice', that is, 'education that provides appropriate stimulating play experiences to enable individual children to progress through defined developmental stages' (Martin 2011, p.135) in which intervention in play was seen as inappropriate. Martin observed that, when children first come into the setting, they learn how to be accepted as a legitimate participant in a community of masculinity or femininity by initially observing the behaviour of those that they have already learnt to identify with, that is, girls or boys.[3] In this nursery, during free play, the children were mainly splitting into separate groups of boys and girls so it was easy for the new children to figure out which activities were appropriate for them and to begin to join in with them and become 'legitimate participants'. The established children actively policed the play borders by telling other children if they were doing something unacceptable for a boy or a girl. Some children wanted to cross these borders and were able to if they were amongst the more confident ones or leaders in their groups, or if they did so out of the public gaze of the other children. For example, one boy was observed washing a doll in the water tray when the other children weren't there. Martin observed that power relations between children were 'key to understanding why boys and girls play in same-sex groups and at different activities' (Martin 2011, p.131). In this particular setting, boys took power and dominated space through football, battle games, including superhero play and construction while girls typically took over home corner role-play areas and skipping. Martin describes an incident where a group of girls took over the yellow climbing frame by calling it 'pink' and joining arms and chanting. Pink was seen by the girls as a symbol of femininity and as a 'pollutant' (Martin 2011, p.131) by the boys. One of Martin's conclusions is that:

> young children often limit their play choices because they need to show other children that they understand the correct behaviour for girls and for boys. They learn that certain ways of behaving will gain them pleasure and recognition, whilst others will bring them hostility and ridicule. (Martin 2011, p.131)

Paechter (2007) explains how similar processes take place in the different contexts of primary and secondary schools. Her explanation of how masculinities and femininities are constructed as oppositional with many consequent gender binaries, such as boys being silly or selfish and girls being sensible or selfless, coming into play was also reflected in the scoping study carried out for the Gender Respect Project. The qualities which appeared in the interviews with the pupils and which are strongly associated with boys or girls (masculinity/ femininity) were: active/passive or decorative; silly/sensible; selfish/ selfless; strong/weak; clever/stupid; brave/scared; and rough/gentle. We were particularly struck by a child who said, 'I'd like to play football but you need lots of training and, like I said on that aeroplane one,[4] you might forget things as well, like if you're shooting a goal you might get it into the wrong goal.' She recognised that training makes you good at something, but still believed that as a girl she might be forgetful, so would therefore fail.

The 'communities of practice' (Paechter 2007), where these dualistic discourses are learnt, are particular to different groups of children in different schools in different places, so it is important for teachers to observe pupils in their own schools and engage them in discussion about the particular ways in which femininities and masculinities are being constructed and to be aware of how other identities such as ethnicity, class, sexuality and disability might intersect with gender.

STEREOTYPE THREAT (SOCIAL IDENTITY THREAT)

Another relevant theory about the development of gender roles is the idea of 'stereotype threat', first posited by social psychologists Steele and Aronson (1995) and explained in detail on the Reducing Stereotype Threat website.[5] 'Stereotype threat refers to being at risk of confirming, as self-characteristic, a negative stereotype about one's group' (Stroessner, Good and Webster 2014). Studies have shown that awareness of others' stereotypes increases dramatically between the ages of six and ten, and that this awareness is a precondition for stereotype threat effects. Stereotype threat is triggered by subtle clues in the environment such as role models, the presence of one's own gender in a particular field such as engineering or pictures and books in a classroom, and has been shown to have an effect not only on self-belief but also on actual ability to do something. For example, in maths tests, women who have had to record their sex at the beginning of a test have done less well in the test than men, whereas where sex has not been recorded they have performed equally well. Just the ticking of a box can trigger stereotype threat and a whole set of negative beliefs about women and mathematical ability:

> Stereotype effects have been seen in women who record their sex at the beginning of a test…are in the minority as they take the test; have just watched women acting in air-headed ways in commercials or have instructors or peers who hold consciously or otherwise – sexist attitudes. (Fine 2010, p.32)

Studies have also shown that men are susceptible to stereotype threat on a test of social sensitivity. In many primary classrooms, although boys and girls aren't necessarily lined up separately, their gender is constantly made salient by teachers and other staff making reference to boys and girls as separate groups and naming the groups as 'boys and girls' rather than 'children', thus potentially triggering stereotype threat.

In the second part of this book I explore how teachers can explicitly engage children in revealing hidden stereotypes. Research has shown that 'in the absence of direct interventions children with highly stereotyped attitudes are likely to distort incoming counter-stereotypical information to make it stereotype consistent thus reinforcing rather than reducing stereotypes' (Liben, Bigler and Krogh 2001, p.358). These direct interventions could involve using such methods as Philosophy for Children (P4C; described with lesson suggestions in Chapter 7) or other dialogic learning approaches to engage children in questioning their assumptions, sharing alternative perspectives, challenging each other and examining the validity of their reasons for a particular view. It is important to provide counter-stereotypical information, alternative role models, historical and global contexts and stories to challenge received norms which reinforce gender inequality, but only if these are engaged with and made sense of in an active way. The advice for 'reducing stereotype threat' which may undermine girls' ability in mathematics and science, or boys' emotional literacy, also includes the importance of revealing the way that stereotype threat operates and opening it up to critical scrutiny: its power is in its subtlety – once someone is aware of its operation, stereotype threat can no longer influence performance (Johns, Schmader and Martens 2005).

SUMMARY

This chapter has:

- – offered some evidence and arguments to counter the idea that gender differences are innate

- – described how gender is socially constructed

- – explored 'stereotype threat'.

Chapter 3

GENDER STEREOTYPING

SPORT AND CAREER CHOICES

*'He's doing work and women can't do the work as well because
they might electrocute themselves but men are much stronger
and they can do it.'*

(Boy, aged seven)

Research has shown that gender stereotyping is alive and well amongst
children in UK primary schools in the 21st century. To find out for
ourselves what views and attitudes children held, we carried out a
scoping study for the Gender Respect Project with focus groups of
children from the schools involved; the results confirmed previous
larger research studies. Teachers involved in the project found
similar views and attitudes in their work with their pupils, and an
activity using the scoping study materials with around 180 pupils
from 15 different primary schools showed similar results three years
running (at workshops at the CRESST (Conflict Resolution Education
in Sheffield Schools Training) Peer Mediators' Conference in January
2015, 2016 and 2017). Two of the areas we focused on, sport and
careers, yielded particularly stark results.

GENDER RESPECT PROJECT SCOPING
STUDY: METHODOLOGY

The scoping study was carried out with the schools involved in the
Gender Respect Project in South Yorkshire between January and
March 2014. There were three primary schools and three secondary
schools located in different parts of Sheffield, a large city in Yorkshire.

The schools have different socio-economic profiles, with one of the primary schools being on the outer edges of the city with mainly White pupils, with very few receiving free school meals (used as a measure of poverty in England, as only children whose parents are on benefits are entitled to receive them). Both of the other primary schools have pupils who are mostly from minority ethnic backgrounds and above-average numbers of pupils receiving free school meals. However, the differences between the schools' intakes didn't seem to have any impact on the attitudes of the pupils in this particular study as we saw consistency of views across all three schools.

Randomly selected, small, single-sex groups of students from each of the schools in the project were interviewed using pictures as a prompt for discussion, with questions covering gender roles (including sport/PE, occupations, expression of emotions and body image), relationships between girls and boys and perceptions of fairness or unfairness (see Appendix 1). The questions were designed to not be leading and the interviewers tried to maintain a friendly but neutral attitude. Follow-up, probing questions such as, 'Some people in society think…what do you think? What has influenced you/changed your mind?', were asked where it was deemed appropriate and fruitful. Although I will focus on the results for the primary-aged pupils below, in total, 50 students were interviewed across the age range 7 to 14. The interviews lasted approximately 30 minutes and were transcribed and analysed.

GENDER RESPECT PROJECT SCOPING STUDY: SPORT AND PE

Across the three primary schools the majority (8 out of 12 boys and 7 out of 12 girls) said that boys were better at football. Only one boy and one girl (in the same school) said that girls and boys are the same at everything and two boys and two girls said it depends on experience and skills. A few mentioned that girls are better at skipping, gymnastics and swimming, with two boys agreeing that girls are good at 'monkey bars and cheerleading' and a boy in another school saying that girls don't do sport but play with 'dolls and stuff'. In all three primary schools both the girls and the boys talked at length about the reasons for these differences, with boys in two of the schools tending to attribute the differences to intrinsic ability (4 out of 12 boys mentioned boys being faster or having more muscles) and the girls across all the schools blaming exclusion and teasing by the boys. In one school the boys were clearly attributing any differences to factors such as practice and interest, which may reflect a growth mindset[1] to learning in the school as a whole. However, it was one of the girls in that school who made the comment about how girls might shoot a football into the wrong goal mentioned in Chapter 2.

In all three primary schools, all of the girls, except for one, who didn't comment, talked about how the negative behaviour of the boys was the main factor in why girls didn't play football. Four of the girls mentioned the boys being too rough and getting into fights and 11 out of 12 mentioned boys excluding girls or saying that they're not good enough to play. Two of the girls in different schools said that boys don't let girls join in because 'they think they're rubbish'. Comments from other girls included:

'Boys don't want girls in their team.'

'Boys say they don't think you'd be any good.'

'They're leaving the girl out because they think the girls can't play basketball because they're just girls.'

'Normally boys say that they can play football and girls can't.'

'Boys are always saying that girls aren't very good but we might be good.'

'Sometimes boys say "aw you're not better at football, we are" and sometimes girls are.'

'Mostly the boys don't let girls play because they think that girls aren't interested.'

'They think they're the boss of us…boys were teasing the other girls who weren't good at it.'

'Boys are more self-centred if they're playing football or something they keep the balls to themselves and they don't let anyone else.'

None of the girls said that they just were *not* interested in playing football although one said she thought boys might *think* girls were not interested (and two of the boys confirmed this). One girl pointed out that boys who choose non-stereotypical sports also receive teasing from other boys:

'In my childminder there's these two boys and one does gymnastics and when C said, "I do gymnastics", B laughed at him because he was a boy and he thought boys don't do gymnastics and it's a silly thing for boys.'

During the interview, one of the boys actually exhibited negative attitudes to girls and football saying such things as 'Seriously, girls playing football!' and mocking the girl in a drawing who is watching the boys play basketball: 'A sad little girl!' Another boy suggested that in the basketball drawing, 'They might be hurting her feelings…and saying, "You're not playing because you're not a boy".'

When we repeated the activity using photographs with mixed groups at the CRESST conference, the experience of exclusion of girls from playground football held true across all 15 schools and was again something which the girls felt very passionate about and the boys agreed was happening.

These findings are consistent with much of previous British research over the last 20 years (see, for example, Thorne 1993; Francis 1998; Skelton and Francis 2003). Paechter (2007, p.100) explains that 'in the British context, masculinity is overwhelmingly constructed through participation in football.' One of the girls in the Gender Respect Project scoping study confirmed this, saying, 'Boys just think about football. It's always on their minds.' Paechter goes on to say that in her own research she found that 'all the dominant boys played, both in and out of school, many every playtime, and had done so since they were very young. Indeed, success at football seems to be central to attaining status within boys' peer groups.' She goes on to suggest that, 'Boys' perception of football as central to dominant masculinity means that girls – and subordinate boys – have either to be excluded or their participation marginalized or downgraded' (Paechter 2007, p.101). A more recent survey of 1500 young people, Changing the Game for Girls, confirmed that girls perceived some boys as being 'over-competitive, inconsiderate and arrogant' (Women's Sport and Fitness Foundation 2012, p.10).

Although clear overall patterns in attitude and experience could be seen through the three primary schools it is important that these don't mask the other responses that didn't fit with these trends. One of the boys maintained his position that: 'We're like the same because boys can do swimming and girls can do swimming and some girls can do boxing…even M plays football.' Later he said, 'I think that girls can still play football. Me and A go to football and there's this girl called L and there's a coach who's a girl and a girls' football team.'

One of the other boys at the same school, who had said that boys are better at football (and consistently noted the differences between men and women), still wished aloud at the end: 'You mostly see the boys on TV in gymnastics as well but you don't really see the girls so you should see the girls in football so there should be like a night: Saturday night for boys, Sunday night for girls.' One of the girls observed how boys may be discouraged from doing things that girls normally did: 'When I played skipping with my friends there was one boy doing it but he went off because no boys were doing it', and another girl suggested that perhaps sometimes girls didn't play football because they were worried about what other girls would think about them.

GENDER RESPECT SCOPING STUDY: OCCUPATIONS AND CAREERS

More than half the girls (8 out of 12) and just under half of the boys (5 out of 12) said they liked the pictures of the men doing childcare and none of them expressed dislike. Even where they saw it as unusual, they thought it was a good thing for men to take care of children. Interestingly enough, when we carried out the activity at the Peer Mediators' Conference, there was quite a strong reaction to the pictures of the men involved in childcare, with some children arguing quite forcefully that 'men aren't good enough to look after babies', 'they don't put enough work in' and 'women want to do it'. Francis (1998) also found this to be the case in her research, concluding that 'the lesser support for the idea of a male child carer compared to children's endorsement of women builders and lorry drivers suggests that equal opportunities discourse has focused on women's ability to perform traditional male jobs' (Francis 1998, p.165). Twenty years later it is interesting that there is still evidence of surprise if not disapproval in relation to evidence of non-gender stereotyped occupations, whether these are men involved in childcare or women involved in construction. In the scoping study, the stronger reactions (of surprise or disapproval/ approval) and more elaborated responses across all the primary schools were towards the pictures of the woman roofer and electrician. The boys' explanations for their disapproval in all three primary schools fitted in with the masculine/feminine binary of 'strong/weak', with several of them taking a protective attitude towards women:

'He's doing work and women can't do the work as well because they might electrocute themselves but men are much stronger and they can do it.' (Boy, aged seven)

'I think boys should do it. It's really dangerous, I'm not being mean but girls aren't as strong as boys and a girl might get an electric shock and have to go to the doctors and she might just fall down and she don't know where she is.' (Boy, aged nine)

'Because how can a woman hold a heavy thing while climbing a ladder...cos she might fall off.' (Boy, aged nine)

'I think men should do it because if ladies fell off they would hurt bad but if men fell off it wouldn't hurt them that bad.' (Boy, aged nine)

Perhaps of even more relevance for this study (because of the possible triggering for the girls of stereotype threat; see Chapter 2) was that several of the girls saw women as less knowledgeable or capable than men (binary of competent/incompetent or clever/stupid).

'Girls are not used to flying planes and everything and sometimes they might not know what they're doing and even if they've had training they might forget or something.' (Girl, aged nine)

'Normally men, they normally fix things and do quite difficult things but instead it's a woman doing it.' (Girl, aged seven)

Table 3.1 Reasons why men and women do different jobs

Reasons given why men and women do different jobs (number of students per reason)	Boy	Girl
Dangerous for women/they get hurt	5	0
Men are stronger	4	2
Women wear jewellery and could get robbed working outside	2	0
Men are more fit	1	0
Women are less capable/less knowledgeable	0	4
Women usually do childcare	2	2
Women are afraid of heights	0	1
Bosses are men so don't let women do jobs	0	1
Women might be made fun of	1	0
Women mostly do housework	2	1

In all three schools many of the male students and some of the female students saw the lack of women in non-stereotyped roles as owing to their intrinsic ability (or lack of ability), with some boys and girls actually disapproving of women's involvement in building and electrical work. However, there were notable exceptions to this trend in two of the schools. One boy consistently took a positive stance towards gender equality, arguing with the others and giving thoughtful reasons and examples from his experiences from home and school:

> 'That can't be true [that women aren't as strong as men] because ladies do cooking. They cook with all those big pots that are heavy and that helps them to become stronger... If you are a lady and you're working at a shop you have to pick up bottles and those big boxes of bicycles and put them on the shelf.' (Boy, aged nine)

He had earlier in the interview said, 'Men have a right to do cooking and to drive a car and ladies have a right to do the same. If men play cricket then ladies can play cricket.' He made reference to Malala, Mandela and Martin Luther King over the course of the interview, making a connection between gender and race equality:

> 'They say that ladies are not allowed to go to school in Pakistan and Syria but if you fight for it like Malala you can... He [Mandela] wanted freedom – White people had about that much [shows with hands] and Black people about that much and they wanted to be equal... When Nelson Mandela and people in America – Martin Luther King – they changed everything and made it equal.'

When asked how he knew about these people, he said that he'd learnt this in assemblies at school and this was confirmed by the project teacher at the school who said that one of the teachers gave very good assemblies on global issues. It may be that school had been able to have such an impact on his ideas because they were reinforced by direct experiences that challenged stereotypes outside of school. The contrast with, particularly the boys' responses, in another school (for example, 'Men are much stronger and they can do it'), where there were also regular assemblies about global equality issues, may have been because of the difference in age of the students (between seven and nine) or perhaps related to their home experiences (or, indeed, other factors which this limited study has been unable to uncover).

Boys in the third school also drew on their own experiences to counter the arguments of the others: 'I disagree with…because some women do pilot jobs. Once I went to my country and saw women driving the aeroplanes, someone working as the pilot.'

Aspirations

The students across all the schools were asked whether they had any idea about what kind of job they would like to do when they grew up, and although this was a small sample it is interesting to see clear patterns in their choices.

Table 3.2 Children's occupational aspirations

Occupation	Boy	Girl
Police officer	2	3
Doctor	1	4
Dentist	1	0
Midwife	0	1
Nurse	0	1
Vet	0	2
Engineer	3	0
Builder	3	0
Game designer	2	0
Electronics	2	1 (computer fixer)
Inventor	1	0
Zookeeper	1	0
Lawyer	0	1
Teacher	0	1
Nursery	0	1
Journalist	0	1
Librarian	0	1
Football player	5	0
Wrestler	1	0
Hairdresser	0	1
Beautician	0	2
Chef	0	2

Farmer	0	1
Firefighter	1	0
Flight attendant	1	0
Taxi driver	1	0
Actor	1	0
Artist	1	0
TV director	1	0
Ice cream man	1	0
Dancer	0	1
Millionaire	1	0

Doctor, police officer and electronics were the only three occupations mentioned by both girls and boys.

Only 9 girls compared to 14 boys chose occupations relating to STEM (Science, Technology, Engineering, Mathematics, highlighted in dark grey in the table). Of those relating to STEM, 8 out of 9 girls chose occupations which could be said to be in the caring professions whereas only 3 out of 14 boys chose occupations which could be said to be involved with caring (for people or animals). Other notable points are the large number of boys who said they wanted to be footballers (highlighted in light grey in the table) and the fact that only girls mentioned the possibility of becoming beauticians or hairdressers, while only boys mentioned becoming builders and engineers. Some of the students gave reasons for their choices and, apart from more obvious reasons such as being good at something or liking to do it, several of the boys mentioned the importance of being able to earn enough money to be able to look after family in the UK and Pakistan, which implies a traditional belief in the responsibility of men to be providers for their families. Francis' (1998) findings were similar with an 'arts/caring trend in the female choices, compared to the sciences/sports trend in the male ones' (p.53). She also notes that:

> few children chose jobs traditionally performed by the opposite sex: one girl chose scientist, one chose film director, one chose fire-fighter, and three chose solicitor. Of the boys, the only one to cross the gender barrier was the boy who chose hairdresser, suggesting that boys may be even less willing to cross occupational gender boundaries than girls. (Francis 1998, p.53)

The findings in both studies fit a stereotypical pattern of career choices of young people post-16:

> Vocational choices, including apprenticeships are heavily gendered and white males predominate in most training provision. Popular choices like construction and plumbing are more than 90 per cent male, with health and social care and hairdressing more than 90 per cent female. (Hutchinson *et al.* 2011, p.vi; see also Fuller and Unwin 2013)

An Ofsted study of girls' career aspirations also found similar patterns and that, where girls did end up choosing non-stereotypical careers, it was because of experiences of 'direct observation of a professional at work, through mentoring activities and through personal encounters and extended discussion with a professional about what their job was actually like' (Ofsted 2011, p.5). The Institute of Physics, in its' *Closing Doors* (2013) study of progression from GCSE to A Level subjects of all students in England, using analysis of the National Pupil Database, found: 'English, biology and psychology have a balance towards "girls" and physics, mathematics and economics towards "boys".'

The Gender Respect Project scoping study results, coupled with evidence from other research and activities to gauge the issues of concern to the children in the project schools, led to the primary project teachers developing and implementing several lessons with a focus on sport and occupations. Accounts of these, with lesson plans, appear in Chapter 7.

SUMMARY

This chapter has:

- given an account of some of the stereotypical views of primary-aged children in relation to sport, occupations and career aspirations based on the Gender Respect Project scoping study.

Chapter 4

RELATIONSHIPS BETWEEN GIRLS AND BOYS

'You should wear that amount of make-up instead of going over the top and looking like a tart.'

(Girl, aged twelve)

Throughout the Gender Respect Project a recurring and troubling theme was how problematic relationships seemed to be between girls and boys both at primary and secondary school level. This was illustrated in the previous chapter in relation to playground football but was also reflected in other parts of the scoping study and during the classroom work with pupils:

'Most boys don't want to play with girls, and boys and girls don't like playing together... Boys in class they don't go anywhere near girls... They'll just ignore the girls.' (Girl, aged nine)

'Sometimes boys are quite horrible to girls... Sometimes girls get upset because boys say they're fat.' (Girl, aged nine)

'I don't want to be friends with girls. I'm used to boys. I'm a boy and I've got different things to say than girls.' (Boy, aged nine)

'I don't like none [photographs showing friendships between girls and boys] because having girlfriends I don't like.' (Boy, aged nine)

'They [the girls] always walk around...they don't listen to us. They just keep on talking.' (Boy, aged nine)

'You can't have a girl and a boy as a friend.' (Boy, aged seven)

'In group work I used to sit with the boys and then everyone started talking.' (Girl, aged twelve)

The separation of children's friendship groups into boys and girls in primary schools, and the negativity which accompanied this, could be seen as forming a foundation for further disrespectful relationships in secondary school where research has found real problems relating to sexual harassment and violence in relationships (discussed below). We know, through previous research, that the heteronormative culture of sexualisation of relationships into boy/girl friends seems to start early, with even four-year-olds making reference to their girl friends. 'Little boys are required to prove that they are "real boys" in ways that mark them masculine, even macho, and therefore (by definition) heterosexual' (Epstein et al. 2001, p.135). Renold's research (2007) shows the ways in which at the other end of primary school 'year 6 boys (ten and eleven years old) engage with, practice, and occupy heterosexualities and…how integral heterosexual performances are to the production of a "real boy"' (p.279).

Two other main issues which were identified by the Gender Respect Project which can be seen to contribute to problematic sexual relationships between girls and boys into adolescence and beyond are the boys' lack of emotional literacy and the objectification of girls and women.

BOYS' LACK OF EMOTIONAL LITERACY

Being able to recognise and talk about feelings is important in any personal relationship as well as for an individual's mental health. Although in the scoping study there was a strong pattern of both boys and girls in the primary and secondary schools thinking men should be able to cry, there was some recognition that it wasn't usual and could provoke teasing. Sixteen out of 25 girls actually said it was okay for men to cry, slightly more than the boys (14 out of 25). Girls in two of the primary schools pointed out that it wasn't normal to see men crying:

'My dad hasn't cried in years.' (Girl, aged seven)

'Normally boys don't cry…but it's not illegal.' (Girl, aged nine)

In two of the primary schools the nine-year-old girls talked more about the danger of being teased if boys cry: 'If they cry people think they're weak and like, tease them'; 'Boys don't really cry because they want to show people that they can be brave.' But another girl pointed out, 'Sometimes you don't want to show them that you want to cry but you need to cry and not hold it in or it gets into your mind.' However, the nine-year-old boys in both of these schools were positive about men crying: 'It would be weird to not cry with sad stuff'; 'When I went to Thornbridge I was really sad and when I got off the phone I started crying'; 'It's nothing to be embarrassed about.' The link between masculinity and heteronormativity could be seen in this comment from a 13-year-old boy: 'I think it would be good if men could express feelings towards other men without being called gay or lesbian when it's not true.' In one of the primary schools and one of the secondary schools, three of the boys were negative about men crying: 'Like they're a wimp'; 'I think girls laugh because once I fell over and girls laughed at me' (boy, aged seven). One 11-year-old boy said, 'If you cry for no reason...not really manly is it?' and proceeded, while giggling, to give an account of a time when a boy had started crying.

OBJECTIFICATION OF GIRLS AND WOMEN'S BODIES

The objectification of girls and women's bodies which they experience through daily interpersonal interaction as well as consumption of multimedia has been shown to have an adverse impact on mental health, being associated with 'self-objectification, habitual body monitoring, body shame, internalization of the thin ideal...and disordered eating among both lesbian and heterosexual women' (Szymanski, Moffitt and Carr 2011, p.11).

In the scoping study it was noticeable that two of the girls in one of the primary schools mentioned body weight and muscle definition in relation to women's bodies. One girl said, 'I don't think she [Jessica Ennis] cares how she looks unless she's fat' and another said, 'I wouldn't want to have a six pack... I wouldn't myself like to have big muscles... I wouldn't want to be fat because people talk behind your back.' Later she confirmed this, 'Sometimes girls get upset because boys say they're fat' (girl, aged nine). A 19-year-old young woman, in an online focus group discussion with six 18- and 19-year-old women in 2017, recalled 'I was calling myself fat by the age of 7' and another agreed, 'Yeah, I would sit on the exercise bike while watching Corrie.' In the Girlguiding 'Girls' Attitudes Survey' (2016) which canvassed the views of 1600 girls and young women aged 7 to 21, 17 per cent of girls aged 7 to 10 felt they should lose weight and this rose to 54 per cent for 11- to 16-year-olds and 66 per cent for 17- to 21-year-olds.

Girls report they are made to feel that how they look is the most important thing about them – something very young girls feel – and this only increases as they get older. They believe their appearance matters when it comes to being successful in life, and that there are double standards for girls compared with boys. 'Over the past five years, we have seen a significant decline in how happy girls feel about their appearance. In 2011, 73% of girls aged 7 to 21 were happy with how they looked, falling to 61% this year' (Girlguiding 2016, p.5).

In the scoping study there was evidence of a very careful monitoring, even policing, of girls' own and others' appearances:

> 'You should wear that amount of make-up instead of going over the top and looking like a tart, because when you put too much on people wouldn't be your friend… We're not girly girls…we know what to wear and everything but it's like what other people are wearing.' (Girl, aged twelve)

The open use of the word 'tart' fits with previous research which has discussed the 'virgin/whore narratives which collectively police behaviour' (Paechter 2007, p.144). Girls still seem to be treading that thin line between being seen as frigid or too easy, and many of them seem to spend a lot of energy ensuring that their appearance doesn't give the 'wrong' messages to boys. One of the Gender Respect Project teachers followed this finding up by surveying the language used to describe girls and boys in her secondary school, and this confirmed the prevalence of negative language towards girls such as 'slag'. A YouGov poll carried out with a representative sample of 788 16- to 18-year-olds in 2010 found that '71% of all 16–18-year-olds (i.e. boys and girls) say they hear sexual name-calling with terms such as "slut" or "slag" towards girls at schools daily or a few times a week' (End Violence Against Women 2017).

The impact of pornography and sexual harassment

The impact of the ubiquitous objectification of girls and women's bodies, combined with a more ready access to pornography, and many boys' lack of emotional literacy and skill at communicating about feelings, make a potentially toxic cocktail for young people in their relationships. Understanding consent can be difficult in these circumstances. For example, Laura Bates, from the Everyday Sexism Project, while talking about the impact of pornography on young people at the Gender Respect – Youth Effect conference (April 2016), described an incident at one school she visited:

> I was in a school where a teacher told me they had recently had a rape case involving a 14-year-old male perpetrator. One of the teachers had asked him, 'Why didn't you stop when she was crying?' and he had replied, 'Because it's normal for girls to cry during sex'. (Also quoted as evidence in House of Commons Women and Equalities Committee 2016)

An Inquiry into Child Sexual Exploitation in Gangs and Groups carried out for the Children's Commissioner of England confirmed Bates' anecdotal evidence, well documented on her 'Everyday Sexism'[1] site:

> The use of and children's access to pornography emerged as a key theme during the first year of the Inquiry. It was mentioned by boys in witness statements after being apprehended for the rape of a child, one of whom said it was 'like being in a porn movie'; we had frequent accounts of both girls' and boys' expectations of sex being drawn from pornography they had seen; and professionals told us troubling stories of the extent to which teenagers and younger children routinely access pornography, including extreme and violent images. We also found compelling evidence that too many boys believe that they have an absolute entitlement to sex at any time, in any place, in any way and with whomever they wish. Equally worryingly, we heard that too often girls feel they have no alternative but to submit to boys' demands, regardless of their own wishes. (Horvath et al. 2011, p.6)

Several other reports have highlighted the problem of sexual harassment for young people in the UK. In the previously cited YouGov poll, nearly a third of 16- to18-year-old girls reported that they had experienced unwanted sexual touching at school and another third said they had regularly seen sexual pictures on mobile phones (End Violence Against Women 2017).

A Qualitative Study of Children, Young People and 'Sexting' carried out for the NSPCC by the Institute of Education (Ringrose *et al.* 2012) discusses, in depth, the research undertaken surrounding 'sexting' and sexual material shared via social media sites and personal mobile phone and messages. BlackBerry Messenger and Facebook played a key role in this. Young people felt pressure to conform and did not feel that they could confide in anyone about what was happening for fear of being called a 'snake' or a 'grass'. Terms they frequently used were 'daggering' (touching from behind) and 'touching up', and they experienced this daily. Young people described sites where boys in particular would 'expose' photos and videos which other young girls had sent them. These sites would degrade women and, after a quick search on Facebook, a Master's student on placement with the Gender Respect Project found various sites such as 'lets expose these hoes'. Young people used the term 'beats or beating' instead of 'having sex' or 'making love', a particularly violent synonym or slang term:

> One of the key findings of this research highlights the extent to which gendered power relations saturate the young people's lives. No understanding of sexting would be complete without an appreciation of the extent to which an often completely normalized sexism constitutes the context for all relationships both on and off-line... deeply rooted notion that girls and young women's bodies are somehow the property of boys and young men...boys' failure to perform a particular kind of macho masculinity carries with it the risk of being labeled 'gay'...'If they had a picture of a girl naked and you told them "That's wrong" they will think straight away you are gay.' (Focus group, Year 10 boy) (Ringrose *et al.* 2012, pp.28, 29, 42, 43)

These issues have also been found with younger children with almost a quarter (24.6%) of young people being 12 years or younger when they first saw pornography online and 7.3 per cent being under 10 (House of Commons Women and Equalities Committee 2016). In a NASUWT survey of 1507 teachers: '62% reported pupils viewing/sharing online sexual content, with one in six (16%) of these children of primary school age' (NASUWT 2017).

According to the written submission from Girlguiding to the same Committee, '22% of girls aged 7–12 had experienced jokes of a sexual nature from boys...12% of girls had seen rude pictures or rude graffiti about girls and women...10% had experienced unwanted touching' (2016, p.7). 'Sexual harassment…"definitely happens in primary school, especially in year 5 and 6", with the activities occurring in years 5–6 listed as "Lifting up skirts and pulling down pants" and "Some kids [being] scared to wear skirts"' (Brook Focus Group in the Wirral submission to House of Commons Women and Equalities Committee 2016). Alice, in the 18- to 19-year-old focus group, said:

> 'I remember a boy in the year below coming up to me and some other girls in, like year five, and naming us all sexist words like "slut", "bitch" and then I was called a "hoe" but I didn't know what that meant and thought he called me a horse and felt lucky, lol.'

Carys, another member of the group, said:

> 'I feel like in primary school everything related to sex can be used as an insult though. I remember one boy coming up to me saying, "You're a virgin", trying to insult me, but clearly not knowing what it meant. But I did, and I was just like "Um, yep" ha-ha. But yeah, literally everything to do with sex and relationships, be it good or bad, seemed bad in primary school and I think that's because nobody told us anything about it, so through lack of knowledge everyone was just hostile towards stuff like that.'

Carys' comment points towards the importance of well thought out Relationships and Sex Education (RSE) in primary schools, and there is plenty of guidance for schools available to ensure this.[2,3]

In Chapter 7 there are examples of PSHE and RSE lesson plans, appropriate for primary-aged children, which take into account these issues of body image, consent and pornography.

Both problems of emotional illiteracy and objectification of girls and women, which relate to hegemonic masculinity and emphasised femininity, have an impact on individual girls and boys as well as their relationships with each other. There were many reports in British and American media at the time of writing this book, about the extent of mental health issues amongst boys and men, with campaigns by people in the public eye such as Prince Harry and the footballer Rio Ferdinand who were applauded for speaking out about how difficult it was for them to handle grief and the importance of men talking about their feelings (see, for example, BBC 2017; Furness 2017; Kennedy 2017; Mettler 2017).

It is also important to find ways of enabling girls and boys to engage in good working relationships with each other in school, ensuring, for example, that they learn to listen to and collaborate with each other in mixed groups and that casually sexist language or comments are challenged throughout the school. Philosophy for Children (P4C) is an effective methodology for building relationships within a class community. Children learn to listen carefully to all members of the group and realise that everyone has something of value to contribute to a discussion about a controversial issue. It also develops critical thinking which can be applied to the information that children engage with through social media and advertising. Because 'caring thinking' and 'critical thinking' are valued equally in P4C, all children, including boys, develop their sensitivity towards their own and others' feelings and learn to articulate their feelings as well as their thoughts. For more on P4C see Chapter 7.

SUMMARY

This chapter has:

- discussed the often problematic nature of relationships between boys and girls in primary schools

- explored the problem of many boys lacking emotional literacy

- identified the way the objectification of girls and women's bodies contributes to problems such as poor body image and lack of respect from boys

- discussed the impact of pornography on children and young people

- identified some of the implications for work in primary schools.

PART 2

IMPLEMENTING GENDER EQUALITY EDUCATION IN PRIMARY SCHOOLS

Introduction to Part 2

This part of the book offers practical ideas for implementing gender equality across a primary school. The acronym ICE usefully sums up all aspects of school life: Implicit or informal curriculum; Curriculum, as in formal, taught curriculum; and Explicit teaching about gender issues. A school policy on gender equality would need to include all aspects of ICE and could, in the UK, fit within a general policy on equalities, with the Equality Act 2010 (see Chapter 1) providing the statutory guidance. This approach enables the different aspects of equality to work as a whole and allows explicit recognition of intersectionality[1] when considering gender equality. A formal, written school policy[2] that is developed with all staff and governors with input from parent representatives supports a whole-school approach to gender equality and provides essential back-up for teachers in the case of any conflict between home and school values.

Chapter 5

IMPLICIT

This chapter explores how being aware of the 'hidden' curriculum, 'the unintended development of personal values and beliefs of learners, teachers and communities; unexpected impact of a curriculum; unforeseen aspects of a learning process' (UNESCO 2017), can contribute towards gender equality in a primary school. Gendered values, attitudes and norms in a school are implicitly conveyed by teachers' expectations and actions; organisational processes; the physical and the language environment; and relationships between adults, adults and children and between children. It is important to work on these different areas of the informal curriculum as well as the formal curriculum (discussed in Chapter 6), as these will form a backdrop to the more active, explicit interventions that are needed to really shift attitudes and thinking (described in Chapter 7). Under each heading I give a short explanation followed by some bullet-pointed guidance and questions to consider. For a primary school gender equality checklist which includes these questions see Appendix 2.

TEACHER EXPECTATIONS AND PUPIL ATTITUDES TO LEARNING

Children interviewed for the Gender Respect Project scoping study were very clear about the gendered expectations of their teachers, particularly the idea of boys being seen by teachers as silly or 'naughty' and girls as sensible. Both the boys and girls in one school talked about how boys got into trouble more than girls. All four girls at this school said that boys got into trouble more because 'boys like always to fight…normally boys shout really loud so boys get into more trouble. Normally girls don't get into trouble' (girl, aged nine) and three of them saw it as a problem that boys get more attention from teachers because of this, one having the wish that 'no one should get extra attention. Sometimes teachers or parents give attention to boys because they're fighting' (girl, aged nine).

The boys at another school were clear about the difference they perceived in how they were treated, with all of them agreeing that girls got more credits than boys and the teachers believed the girls more than the boys: 'Not like naughty girls only like right good girls' (boy, aged nine). The responses of one of the girls and one of the boys in the third school (younger students, aged seven) reinforced this silly/sensible binary with the boy saying, 'Girls are normally gooder than boys because boys are normally naughty.' The girl felt it was unfair that she was expected to be good: 'Most boys are normally, people think they're quite naughty, so I think people would expect me to be good' (girl, aged seven). A boy in one of the schools felt it was unfair that teachers seemed to develop friendlier relationships with the girls: 'A lot of girl teachers, they don't talk to boys but with girls they are talking all the time' (boy, aged nine).

The perceptions of the students from the project schools seems to be consistent with previous research where it has been found that:

> boys were perceived by their teachers as more likely to exhibit poor concentration in the fidgety sense, of not seeming to be able to sit still. They were believed to be more immature, to have poor behaviour and poor motivation. (Jones and Myhill 2004, p.539)

Research has also shown that teachers' views are noticed by their students:

> certainly pupils' perceptions of teachers are that they have different expectations of boys and girls in terms of their behaviour, the quality of their written work, and the extent to which they punish and praise boys as against girls. (Warrington, Younger and McLellan 2003, p.146)

> For example, our research into 7–8 year old pupils' perceptions of the importance of the gender of their teacher highlighted many instances where teachers used gender as a means of motivating children or controlling children's behaviour. These included, for instance, boys

being seen as particularly keen on IT and maths, and girls at literacy and presentational aspects, and using these aspects to motivate particular gender groups of pupils. (Skelton *et al.* 2007, p.48)

In addition to the evidence that teachers have different expectations of girls and boys' behaviour, research has shown that teachers have different expectations of girls and boys' achievement in different subjects. Cimpian and colleagues' (2016) study on gender gaps in mathematics in the US found that 'females are uniformly underrated relative to their academically and behaviourally similar male peers' (p.15), and suggested that this was one of the contributing factors to their relative underachievement. Other studies have suggested the ways in which teachers' 'differential perception of girls as achieving through hard work and boys as innately clever' (Skelton and Francis 2003, p.8) is communicated to children through their emotional responses and feedback to children, with teachers praising boys for innate ability and girls for effort. This either reflects or reinforces pupils' well-documented, own attitudes towards their learning. Research has shown that:

> girls (are) far more likely to underestimate their performance in a given task than boys and interpret failure in different ways. Boys would accord their failing to lack of effort or blame, apparent inadequacies of external factors such as exams or teachers whilst girls tended to blame themselves, attributing failure to lack of ability. (Skelton and Francis 2003, p.10)

Both attitudes are problematic in different ways. The tendency for boys to see achievement as being related to innate ability can mean that they underrate the importance of hard work and therefore do less well than girls in tests, whereas for many girls their lack of self-belief can be very undermining of their confidence and therefore capability. Many schools in recent years have tried to counteract this 'fixed mindset' by developing a 'growth mindset'[1] to learning in their pupils. It is important that the learning culture of a school emphasises that success is achieved through determination and hard work rather than innate ability, but paradoxically there may need to be some compensatory work with girls to persuade them that they do have innate capabilities equal to others as well.

The results of the present study suggest that teachers should balance between feedback of individual children's innate ability and effort in math and reading, and give their students the feeling of both competency and diligence (Craven, Marsh, & Debus 1991), as well as a mastery orientation and incremental views of abilities (Kamins & Dweck 1999). (Upadyaya and Eccles 2014, p.96)

A healthier growth mindset can be encouraged with what Dweck calls 'process praise,' that encourages perseverance, hard work and accepting challenge. 'This was a tough assignment, but you stuck to it.' 'You had to work really hard, but it paid off.' (Miracle 2015)

There is also evidence that if you teach students about growth mindset, then they are less likely to be influenced by stereotype threat. Dweck (2008) writes in her *Brainology* essay:

negatively stereotyped students (such as girls in math, or African-American and Hispanic students in math and verbal areas) showed substantial benefits from being in a growth-mindset workshop. Stereotypes are typically fixed-mindset labels. They imply that the trait or ability in question is fixed and that some groups have it and others don't. Much of the harm that stereotypes do comes from the fixed-mindset message they send. The growth-mindset, while not denying that performance differences might exist, portrays abilities as acquirable and sends a particularly encouraging message to students who have been negatively stereotyped – one that they respond to with renewed motivation and engagement.

Even where teachers are consciously trying to be fair in their treatment of girls and boys in the primary classroom, given the prevalence of gender-based stereotyping in society it is highly unlikely that anyone would be free of unconscious assumptions which affect their behaviour. The ubiquity of unconscious bias has been well documented in the last 20 years by American psychologists and this understanding is now entering the mainstream in the UK (see, for example, BBC Radio 4 2017). In fact, the Institute of Physics (2015), in its *Opening Doors* guidance, suggests that all secondary teachers school receive unconscious bias training. When I tried out Harvard University's online Implicit Association Test (IAT)[2] on the association of women with family and men with careers, I wasn't surprised to find that I had a 'moderate bias' towards this particular association.

Suggestions and questions

- Are you aware of your own gendered expectations of behaviour and learning?

- Do you expect girls to behave better than boys? Do you disapprove of misbehaving girls more than you disapprove of misbehaving boys?

- Do you reward and sanction behaviour differently depending on the gender of the child?

- How do you use praise and compliments? Do you compliment boys on their appearance as much as girls or for the presentation of their work? Do you praise girls as well as boys for their ability or skills?

- Is there a gender bias in the amount of attention from adults given to children in your classroom? Consider the reasons for the attention and then try out interventions to affect change if appropriate.

- Consider offering praise for hard work and attitude to learning to all children to encourage a 'growth mindset'.

- Consider trying out the Harvard IAT to test out your own unconscious bias.

- Introduce unconscious bias to other members of staff in a staff meeting, giving a chance for members of staff who claim to treat all children the same to have a go with this.

LANGUAGE

Language is an area where people often feel uncertain and ask for guidance or are resistant and refuse to acknowledge its importance. Additionally, many people still refer to political correctness (PC) as an argument against making language adjustments. It is used to trivialise attempts to make language less discriminatory and more inclusive (for a history of the term, see Weigel 2016). Dominant language norms are hard to change but important to challenge as they can provide a subtle reinforcement of gender bias. Several aspects of language are important foci of work on the hidden curriculum in primary schools: the way language is used to reinforce binary gender categories; the way language can reinforce masculine dominance; and how the use of language can implicitly exclude women and girls.

Lining up girls and boys separately (or boy, girl, boy, girl) is now more unusual in primary schools but children are still commonly referred to as boys and girls rather than non-gendered terms such as 'students', 'kids', 'children', 'class', 'the name of the class', 'munchkins' (or other gender-neutral terms of endearment!), 'folks', 'everyone', 'all of you'.[3] A constant reference to gender not only reinforces the idea of rigid separate categories but also potentially induces stereotype threat by making gender salient (see Chapter 2, 'Stereotype Threat').

If the adults who work with young children, through their use of language and their day-to-day interactions with the children, convey the message that gender is an important distinction and furthermore is a binary category with no movement between the two sub-categories, female and male, it ought not to surprise us that young children may begin to develop the same view of gender (Browne 2004).

It is important that thought is given not just to spoken words but also to written or pictorial communication being gender-neutral or inclusive if possible too, such as checking the labels of roles in school: headteacher rather than headmaster or mistress and dinner or lunchtime supervisor rather than dinnerlady and chair or chairperson of governors. Are we conscious of using gender-neutral versions of other occupations such as firefighter, police officer and flight attendant? Do we talk about 'staffing' a desk or stall rather than 'manning' one? Do we talk about people, humanity or humankind instead of man and mankind? Can we use the word artificial or built instead of 'man made'? Do we refer to adult women as 'women' rather than 'girls' or 'ladies' (or if we are using 'ladies', do we also say 'gentlemen')? Can we make 'woman' or 'women' an acceptable and polite term of reference by using it as such, rather than substituting 'lady' when we are talking to young children? Do we allow women teachers in school to be called by the title they have chosen such as Ms rather than defaulting to Miss or Mrs? Perhaps the use of the first names of staff would solve the problem of finding gender-neutral titles.

A less obvious area to focus on is the casual use of the pronoun 'he' when giving an account or explanation. We tend to notice if someone uses 'she' as this still stands out as different. When referring to animals or non-human cartoon/story characters it is worth noticing whether we have a tendency to use 'he' rather than 'she' or the more neutral 'they'. The English language traditionally used 'he' to include women and men but over the last 30 years or so an awareness has developed of how this exclusion of the explicitly female can have a subtle and drip-by-drip effect on how girls and women feel about themselves.

Sometimes it is necessary to challenge the use of overtly sexist language by adults or children. Phrases such as 'man-up' or 'like a girl' or even 'tomboy' imply fixed gender characteristics as belonging to girls or boys. 'Man-up', even when referred to women, implies that it is men rather than women that exhibit the characteristics of bravery and strength and even that there is the normative implication that they *should* be brave. 'Like a girl' when used in phrases like 'throw like a girl' or 'run like a girl' has the negative meaning of throwing or running incompetently. 'Tomboy' implies that when a girl shows interests or acts in ways that are traditionally associated with boys then she is a kind of boy. Interestingly it is still more acceptable for a girl to be called a tomboy than for a boy to be called a 'sissy' or other word that implies femininity, but all should be questioned. Even the labels of 'girly girl' or 'sporty girl' heard as self-definitions by 11-year-olds during the Gender Respect Project scoping study ('We're like girly girls – we don't like rugby') restricts a girl's individual possibilities and choices.

Suggestions and questions

- Try not to refer to pupils as girls or boys – use other non-gender specific collective nouns such as 'children' or 'everyone' or 'class' instead.

- If you need to select small groups of children to line up at the door, for example, then use different categories, such as – 'all those with a birthday from January to June', 'everyone with black shoes', 'line up if your favourite food is...', etc.

- Check that all staff are using gender-neutral spoken and written language – perhaps create a language style guide for your school to support everyone's use of this.

- Challenge sexist language or statements if you hear them, for example, generalisations such as all girls...all boys...the use of girl as an insult, etc.

PHYSICAL ENVIRONMENT AND RESOURCES

Perhaps the easiest, yet still very important, change to make in any institution is the actual physical environment itself – the displays, posters, pictures, photographs, signs, language on the walls and the books and resources in the classrooms and libraries. Some classrooms in schools show a lack of awareness about gender equality in the environment:

Photograph taken by the author in a primary school in North East England, June 2015

Others go out of their way to challenge stereotyping and provide positive role models across gender and ethnicity, as with these posters especially commissioned by a primary school in Sheffield to support their work on Building Learning Power (Claxton 2002).

Pye Bank Primary School, Sheffield. Artist: Andrew Smith

For a detailed environmental checklist see Appendix 2.

Suggestions and questions

- Is there a clear welcome message in the entrance hall/on the outside of the building which states the school's principles on equality and diversity?

- Looked at overall, is there an equal representation of women and men or boys and girls on the walls of the school, paying particular attention to the entrance area?

- Do the images show men, women, girls and boys in a variety of roles, with, for example, girls/women being shown as active and boys/men as caring?

- Is a diverse range of families portrayed?

- How is colour (pink and blue) used in classrooms and corridors? What colours and images are used on coat pegs and name cards?

- Does the language displayed around the school conform to your language style guide?

- Are classroom resources gender stereotyped or segregated in any way (for example, boxes of books for girls and for boys)? What about wet playtime materials – do these give out messages which are counter to gender equality?

- Are the play materials for younger children gender-neutral? How are they organised to enable children to play in areas which might normally be dominated by boys or girls (for example, construction by boys and role-play by girls)?

- What books are included in the school or class libraries? Could older students be involved in auditing books to check for gender bias? Should more books that challenge gender stereotypes be included (for a list of suggested books see Appendix 4).

- Uniform/dress code – would it be possible for the school's uniform or dress code to be gender-neutral? This might mean allowing trousers/leggings/shorts for all genders rather than specifying a school uniform skirt or summer dress for girls, for example.

RELATIONSHIPS AND ROLES

A school which has a strong, positive ethos of mutual respect between all members of its community is in the best position to address any issues related to gender (or other equality or inclusion issue), both amongst staff and amongst students. In primary schools, good leadership is absolutely vital to ensuring this, as headteachers (in particular) and senior leadership teams (SLTs) have a huge influence on what are usually relatively small organisations. Creating a culture of respect between students requires respectful relationships between all staff and between staff and students. Assuming that a school is working together as a community on developing and ensuring mutual respect, it is important to consider the specific gender-related issues it might need to address.

Positive relationships between staff and pupils can sometimes be forged at the expense of gender equality. It is interesting that research shows how male teachers may relate to groups of boys by engaging in banter with them about football: 'Some teachers performed a "laddish" masculinity which was aligned with that of the boys they taught and involved the marginalization and teasing of girls, especially through the mutual valorization of football' (Paechter 2007, p.84). Of course this also marginalises boys who don't conform to this dominant form of masculinity. This issue also connects with the need to consider the modelling of masculinities and femininities by members of school staff. Stephen, a nursery teacher on the Gender Respect Project, made sure that, in his setting, both men and women were involved in caring and disciplinary roles:

> female staff can help male staff by helping to get across the caring side of male staff to pupils and male staff can help by getting across the message that female staff are more than capable of taking a lead on behavioral issues. (Gender Respect Project blog 2014)

Suggestions and questions

- Is there a culture of mutual respect across the whole school community?

- What is the gender balance of different roles in your school? How many male teachers work with younger children and how many female teachers are in management positions?

- Are the cleaners all female but the caretaker/janitor male?

- Can you invite visitors into school (for assemblies, lessons, etc.) who are in roles/occupations that don't conform to gender stereotypes (for example, man who is a full-time parent; men involved in social care, nursing or the arts; female scientists, engineers, builders, firefighters, etc.)?

- Are all staff, including lunchtime supervisors, aware of and have received training on the school's policies on gender equality and diversity?

- Are pupil roles in school gender-balanced? Are boys involved equally with girls in caring and tidying? Are girls expected, equally with boys, to be spokespeople?

- In class group work do girls and boys mix? Are girls as likely as boys to take leadership roles? If not, consider allocating mixed gender groups and assigning roles in the group which are changed regularly (for example, as in 'Reciprocal Reading':[4] summariser, questioner, clarifier, predictor).

- Are teachers and others who work directly with students in the school aware of how they are modelling femininities and masculinities and how they relate to different genders?

- Are visitors who are invited to contribute to assemblies or workshops aware of the school's gender equality policies? Is the headteacher or other teachers able to challenge any practices which go against these (for example, unnecessarily segregating by gender or stereotyping)?

PLAYTIME AND PLAYGROUNDS

Chapter 3 referred to the Gender Respect Project's experience of girls talking about how boys dominated playground spaces with football and how this had been well documented in previous research on playground cultures. Paechter discusses the impact on girls of a conventional feminine expectation that as they get older, sitting and talking is more important to them than being physically active: 'In particular, it inhibits the formation of active and physically assertive femininities' (Paechter 2007, p.98). She goes on to advise, 'Do not assume that girls "just naturally" only want to sit and talk as they grow older. Given appropriate equipment and encouragement many will continue playing through puberty and beyond' (2007, p.109). School playgrounds dominated by boys' football also marginalise those boys who do not conform to hegemonic forms of masculinity but would rather play less physical games.

Suggestions and questions

- How is the playground space used in your school? Involve students in conducting observations and surveys if this is unknown.

- Is the outdoor area designed in such a way as to allow other activities apart from football? Are there areas where other physical activities (such as climbing or skipping) can be engaged in? Are there quiet areas available inside and outside at playtime?

- Is there a need for specific coaching of those children who lack the skills to be able to successfully join in with football or skipping in the playground?

- Does the space need to be timetabled sometimes to promote equality, for example, with girls-only football? (Care needs to be taken with this to find ways of enabling the girls to take up space without reinforcing gender binaries.)

- Are the staff that supervise play time and lunch times trained to teach and facilitate a variety of playground games?

- Is there attractive equipment, apart from footballs, available for children to use in the playground?

EXTRA-CURRICULAR ACTIVITIES

By extra-curricular activities I am referring to all the structured activities in a school that fall outside the taught formal curriculum. This includes clubs, assemblies, celebratory events and non-uniform days.

Since they are optional, it is easy for after-school or lunchtime clubs to become gender-segregated in primary schools. This is particularly a problem if the activities are defined in a traditional way (dance club, football, crafts, etc.) or the gender balance is unmonitored. Adrian, a teacher on the Gender Respect Project, was involved in renaming their clubs with questions to encourage children of all genders to join in:

- Do you know self-defence? (Karate)

- Can you pass a ball to score hoops? (Basketball)

- How can you express yourself through art? (Art)

- Can you control a ball with a racket? (Tennis)

- Can you pass a ball to score goals? (Football)

He also instigated sign-up lists with an equal number of places for girls and boys for each activity to encourage both to join in, although this then presents the potential problem of excluding trans or non-binary children. Perhaps he could have considered the marketing of the activities to ensure an equal number of all genders signed up, particularly thinking about the use of images of children of different genders doing the activities.

The children at another of the Gender Respect Project schools identified the problem of boys not seeing dance as something that they should be involved in and decided to initiate a very successful boys' dance competition to raise the profile of dance for boys.

Suggestions and questions

- Monitor the gender make-up of extra-curricular activities in school (particularly focusing on those that could more traditionally be gender-segregated, like gymnastics, dance and football).

- Consider changing the activities or renaming them if they are gender-segregated or dominated by one particular gender.

- Are school sports/gymnastics teams mixed or single sex or do children have the opportunity to participate in either? If the football teams are single sex, does the girls' team get as much praise and publicity in the school as the boys'?

- How are boys encouraged and enabled to join in with dance, gymnastics, cooking, etc.? Which staff lead these activities and do these conform to gender stereotypes?

- Celebratory assemblies – who gets certificates/awards/praise, etc. for what? (For example, does it need to be one girl and one boy from each class every week thus reinforcing gender binaries – perhaps just the class teacher needs to keep the balance in mind over a period of time?)

- Adults' role modelling – consider which characters from a book you are dressing up as for World Book Day or other dressing up days – use these as an opportunity to challenge gender stereotypes, portray strong girls, sensitive boys and so on.

- School proms/discos – would calling it the 'leavers' party' rather than the 'prom', which has heteronormative connotations, alleviate the pressures to conform to gendered expectations in dress and behaviour?[5] Do the letters home about these events actively encourage girls to wear their prettiest dresses, etc.?

PARTNERSHIPS WITH PARENTS, CARERS AND FAMILIES

The reasons and principles for engaging and working in partnership with parents and families are the same for any area of school life and there is wide recognition within primary schools of its central importance for children's learning and well being. This partnership is even more essential in relation to more controversial equality issues, particularly where school and home values may be out of alignment. So, in addition to ensuring that the principles of gender equality permeate relationships between home and school, most schools will need to address potential conflicts between different views of the importance and meaning of gender equality, taking into account possible genuine sensitivities relating to religious and cultural practices.

Suggestions and questions

Incorporating gender equality into relationships with parents and families:

- Communication about and with parents and carers – avoid referring to 'mums' and 'dads'.

- Ensure that school-based, parent and child clubs are gender-inclusive so that, for example, male carers feel welcome and comfortable.

- Ensure that arrangements for discussions with parents and carers include everyone and reflect complex working patterns.

- Display photographs of fathers as well as mothers engaged in work or projects in the school.

- Make sure your displays reflect the make-up of your families, including single and same-sex parents.

Communicating with and engaging parents in gender equality work in school:

- Provide opportunities for parents/carers to learn about policies and practices in the school in relation to gender equality – enable open, non-judgemental discussions where parents/carers can talk about their concerns and areas of agreement/disagreement.

- Communicate gender equality practices through news-letters, school website, letters home and social media (blogs, Twitter, etc.).

- Be prepared for challenging situations: ensure there is senior management support for class teachers. Work on possible scenarios/actual scenarios in staff meetings so everyone is prepared to respond to challenges. Discussion of gender equality can reveal prejudices and fears in relation to sexuality, so how to tackle this will also need to be an important consideration. Moffat (2016) provides useful experience and guidance on LGBT+ equality in primary schools.

SOME POSSIBLE SCENARIOS

Some possible scenarios for staff to consider how they might respond:

1. 'It says in your brochure something about equal opportunities and gender. What exactly does that mean?'

2. 'I don't want you to let my son do this needlework stuff. He's a boy; he should be playing with cars and trains, not doing embroidery. Are you trying to turn them into wimps?'

3. 'Tasha's gran has been going on about your clambering frame. She has a thing about girls falling on their privates; she stopped my wife climbing when she was young. Is it dangerous?'

4. 'I know all this gender stuff is very politically correct – very feminist and all that. But I think you should keep politics out of the nursery. They're innocent little children and you're trying to brainwash them.'

5. 'I don't really mind Jon playing with the dolls, because he's very young still. But his dad's really uncomfortable about it. What happens when he's a bit older, will you do football and things with him?'

6. 'I agree that children learn very young. But they should be learning what will help them when they are grown up. And that means learning how to behave like a proper young lady or young man' (Lindon 2006, p.244).

SUMMARY

This chapter has:

– provided some guidance on how the implicit or hidden learning and teaching that happens in primary schools can promote gender equality.

Chapter 6

CURRICULUM

For real change it is important to examine everything that happens in schools through a gender equality lens, and this includes the taught curriculum. The key question is: how can the content of the curriculum include all genders without appealing to and therefore reinforcing gender stereotypes? Over the last 30 years feminist research has unearthed important women in all fields and from all backgrounds who had been previously lost in a patriarchal interpretation of history. Yet, even today in the UK, as a young woman in the Sounds Familiar survey said, 'In the curriculum you hardly ever hear about any women and if a person of colour is mentioned it's never a woman' (Taafe 2017, p.7).

In research conducted for the Women's Sport and Fitness Foundation surveying 1500 young people in the UK, 43 per cent of secondary-age respondents agreed 'there aren't many sporting role models for girls' (2012, p.4). Even in fields which have been seen to be more accessible to girls at a school level such as the arts, humanities and even food technology (cooking), famous men tend to be better known than famous women in spite of the fact that it is now very easy to find many examples in all fields just using an internet search.

There has been particular concern in recent years about the, still low, participation of girls and women in STEM in post-16 study and in occupations. 'By the age of 15, 51 out of 54 countries in PISA 2006 had a statistically significant difference in the proportion of boys and girls planning a career in engineering or computing, all towards boys' (Smith 2014, p.3).

There are three common factors which have been found to influence choice of STEM subjects usefully summed up by Zecharia and colleagues as:

1. Relevance of STEM = Is it for people like me?

2. Perceived actual and relative ability = Do I feel confident?

3. Science capital = Can I see the possibilities and pathways?

(Zecharia *et al.* 2014, p.9)

Research into participation in maths has identified 'enjoyment' as another reason particularly important for girls (Smith 2014).

In relation to 'Is it for people like me?' much has been written about how existing STEM and gender stereotypes affect girls' participation. Research has shown that girls who define themselves as 'girly' at age 10–11 were less likely to have STEM-related career aspirations and unlikely to persist with them by age 12–13. In addition to this, 'The factors which hinder students from developing science aspirations are amplified in the case of Black students, due to the multiple inequalities they face. This means that science aspirations are particularly precarious among these students' (ASPIRES 2013, p.3).

> Representations of mathematicians are associated with maleness, Whiteness, middle-classness and heterosexuality. They are allied with heroism and unusual natural intelligence, as in the Bletchley Park code breakers, but also with fragility and social competence. There is a relatively new media image of young, attractive women 'geeks' that contrast with the old, male image of mathematics. (Smith 2014, p.16)

The STEM careers themselves are often thought of as all about 'heavy machinery and oily overalls' (Zecharia *et al.* 2014, p.10). Zecharia and colleagues argue that we should be promoting:

> more realistic representations of what STEM careers actually entail, and how creative they can be… We believe that 'Making the world a better place' is a value-based career choice that appeals to boys and girls. By not embedding the creative potential and real world value of STEM careers into teaching we are missing an entire demographic – not just girls. (2014, p.20)

> Any messaging should break down the 'masculine' STEM stereotype and the narrow male and female gender stereotypes to focus on STEM being for everyone. (Campaign for Science and Engineering 2014, p.30)

One of the recommendations from the Institute of Physics (2015) for changing school cultures so that girls and boys are able to make non-gender-stereotyped subject choices later on in their schooling was that subject areas should be treated equally by the school. Science (particularly physics and chemistry) and mathematics being seen as more important and also harder than other subjects has been shown to have a detrimental effect on girls' confidence in those subjects (PISA 2015). Although, as only English, maths and, in some cases, science are assessed in the SATs which children sit at the end of primary school, it is quite a challenge to put an equal emphasis on all subjects, and teachers can take care not to denigrate other subjects or to imply that they are easier or that they, themselves, find them easier or harder. In the spirit of treating subjects equally I have listed subjects below separately in alphabetical order with some questions for consideration, general guidance and links to useful websites.[1]

ART AND DESIGN

The National Curriculum in England Key Stages 1 and 2 gives a useful summary of the purpose of art and design:

> A high-quality art and design education should engage, inspire and challenge pupils, equipping them with the knowledge and skills to experiment, invent and create their own works of art, craft and design. As pupils progress, they should be able to think critically and develop a more rigorous understanding of art and design. They should also know how art and design both reflect and shape our history, and contribute to the culture, creativity and wealth of our nation. (DfE 2013, p.176)

When studying historical and contemporary works of art it is impossible to ignore gender issues as art can be seen as reflecting, commenting on and reinventing society. Historical gender relations and roles can be studied through works of art from previous centuries. Contemporary feminist art can provoke discussion about gender equality issues. The study of historical female artists such as Artemisia Gentileschi can highlight not only that there were well-known female artists historically, but also how knowledge of these artists has been buried at certain times in history. This raises issues about societal views of the role of women and who has the power to decide who should be included in the canon of 'great artists'. Gender issues also need to be considered when children are designing and making art, ensuring that all children, regardless of gender, have equal access to materials and skills development, and that topics chosen for art are not biased towards a particular gender.

Questions and suggestions

- When given free choice, who uses the art materials in your classroom and how are they used? Are girls more likely to draw, paint or colour or be involved in more detailed work and are boys more likely to engage in large construction or 3D materials such as clay?

- Consider how you might ensure that all students are developing a full range of artistic skills.

- Find out whether your students associate the word 'artist' with men or women. Is fashion and textiles art more associated with women?

- Ask your students whether they associate particular colours with men or women.

- Do you and your students know as many female artists as male artists?

Resources

- The Tate Gallery Kids area provides several examples of women artists for students to explore including Georgia O'Keefe, Bridget Riley and Sheela Gowda:

  www.tate.org.uk/kids/explore/kids-view/explore-georgia-okeeffe

  www.tate.org.uk/kids/explore/who-is/who-bridget-riley

  www.tate.org.uk/kids/explore/who-is/who-sheela-gowda.

- Another link at the Tate explores The Guerrilla Girls (www.tate. org.uk/kids/explore/who-is/who-are-guerrilla-girls), a group of anonymous women artists who have been protesting against racism and sexism in the art world since the 1980s.

- The Tate gallery quiz 'Which art superhero are you?' is a series of multiple choice questions illustrated by works of art and would extend the idea of superheroes in such a topic. Plenty of women artists and artists from around the world are included: www.tate.org.uk/kids/games-quizzes/quiz-which-art-superhero-are-you.

- Moma, the Museum of Modern Art in New York, has activities and PowerPoints relating to the theme of identity on its website: www.moma.org/learn/moma_learning/tools_tips.

- For information about Artemesia Gentileschi, a 17th century artist, well-known in her time, but then obscured from history until more recently, go to www.artemisia-gentileschi.com.

- Several books are available for children about women artists (see Appendix 4 for a list of books).

COMPUTING

The uptake by young women of computer science at A level in England is around 10 per cent of the total number of students (McDonald 2017), and there are concerns that the loss of the broader subject of Information and Communications Technology (ICT) will impact on girls' general engagement in the subject (since 2014 'computing' has been substituted for ICT in the primary curriculum in England). The early focus on computing skills may increase the uptake of computer science of all students later on in their school careers, but only if the stereotypes associated with computing as being for 'male geeks' are overcome from an early age.

Peter Kemp, from Roehampton University, who is involved in writing *The Annual Computing Education Report*, comments:

Computing is all around us, it has a big impact in the way the world works and it's important that students have a good understanding of the world we live in. There are multiple groups – especially girls – with poor access to computing qualifications and steps need to be taken to increase accessibility of the subject and encourage students to appreciate its value. (University of Roehampton 2016)

Questions and suggestions

- Do you communicate to students that computing is creative and fun?

- Provide information about women involved in computing, for example, women's involvement at the beginning (Ada Lovelace, Grace Hopper and Dorothy Vaughan) and current famous women involved in computer science (such as Dame Wendy Hall, Professor of Computer Science at University of Southampton).

- Carefully consider whether computing project topics appeal to all genders without stereotyping.

Resources

- www.geekgurldiaries.co.uk – '…a collection of video logs about using and making technology, alongside interviews with inspirational women in the fields of computing, science, technology and engineering. They also include video contributions from women working in IT and Science, and include "Geek Gurl Diaries On Air" panel discussions with graduate computer science students on various topics like computer gaming and geek culture.'

DESIGN AND TECHNOLOGY (D&T)

At GCSE there is a marked tendency towards stereotypical subject choices within design and technology in England, with electronic products having an intake of 95 per cent boys and resistant materials having around 85 per cent boys, but with boys making up about 4 per cent of students studying textiles and 35 per cent of those studying food technology (Bramley, Vidal Rodeiro and Vitello 2015, p.12). Primary schools can contribute to the prevention of the development of these stereotypical associations of boys with certain subjects and girls with others by taking positive counter-stereotypical measures such as those suggested below.

Questions and suggestions

- In Early Years, are construction materials and other play materials associated with D&T played with equally by girls as well as boys and presented in gender-neutral ways?

- Are all genders equally comfortable with the different aspects of D&T?

- Are all aspects of D&T portrayed by staff and the school as equally relevant to girls and boys?

- Are skills gaps identified and extra support given where needed? Would it be helpful to have cookery and textiles clubs that boys are encouraged to attend and electronic or resistant materials clubs where girls are actively invited?

- Are D&T tasks described in gender-inclusive or counter-stereotyped ways?

- Are the contributions of both men and women to the subject recognised?

- Could visitors be invited into the classroom as counter-stereotypical role models (for example, female chef not cook; female engineers)?

Resources

- www.stem.org.uk/resources/collection/4372/inspiring-scientists – Case studies of current British scientists with minority ethnic heritage. Each resource has a film of the scientist talking about their work and a timeline of their life and a STEM lesson plan for primary and secondary age groups.

- www.wes.org.uk – The Women's Engineering Society, case studies of women in engineering with films.

- www.westskills.org.uk/stories – 'Women in Science, Engineering and Technology', based in Sheffield with case studies of local women working in construction and engineering and workshops in schools.

- www.practicalaction.org/schools – Free teaching materials which give a real world global context to STEM and help to break down the narrow stereotypes about STEM careers.

ENGLISH LANGUAGE AND LITERACY

As explained in Chapter 1 there is genuine concern over the significant (6%) gap between boys' and girls' attainment in literacy in English KS2 SATs. However, interventions which have highlighted perceived gender differences, such as using 'boy-friendly' books, have largely failed to narrow the gap while reinforcing harmful stereotypes. Much of the literature points to the importance of providing excellent quality teaching and learning opportunities in schools for all pupils. The questions and suggestions below specifically address the issue of gender stereotyping and ensuring equality of participation in English by all pupils, regardless of gender.

Questions and suggestions

- Is there gender differentiation in the amount of classroom talk engaged in by girls and boys? Consider monitoring the type and quality of verbal contributions by gender.

- Do teachers call on boys more than girls to answer questions? Consider randomising who gets chosen by drawing lollipop sticks or balls with names on.

- See Chapter 7 for an explanation of Philosophy for Children (P4C), an approach to dialogic learning and teaching which can contribute considerably to the development of all pupils' speaking and listening skills.

- How does your classroom challenge assumptions about gendered text preferences, for example, that boys prefer non-fiction to fiction and girls avoid fantasy or science fiction;

that boys like writing short stories full of action and girls prefer not to take risks in their writing but like to write at length?

- Review the literature that you read to children and that is available in your classroom for children to read independently.

Resources

- For a checklist to analyse books with gender equality in mind see Appendix 3 and for a list of recommended children's books see Appendix 4.

GEOGRAPHY

In geography children learn about how different people across the world live together and interact with their environments. From a gender equality perspective it can enable children to be inspired by examples of gender-equal societies as well as the global prevalence of gender inequality, which led to Sustainable Development Goal 5: 'Achieve gender equality and empower all girls' (UN 2017). With global as well as local examples of ways of life, it is important, in geography, to avoid gender stereotyping and to be aware of and help children to challenge any assumptions that they might hold about gender relations in distant places.

Questions and suggestions

- Do you include examples of men/women in different roles across the world – for example, female farmers?

- Do you make a distinction between paid and unpaid work – recognising work in the home as equally valuable?

- Do women and people of minority ethnic heritage in positions of power and authority feature in your curriculum?

- When looking at leisure activities are women, as well as men, portrayed in active leisure pursuits?

- Fieldwork and practical work on sustainability in the school – are all boys as well as girls involved in, for example, recycling projects in the school?

Resources

- Arwa Amba – An inspiring, positive example of a gender-equal society in the Global South (Ethiopia), www.gender respect2013.wordpress.com/teaching-ideas/arwa-amba. The Gender Respect Wordpress site includes audio interviews about gender equality with members of the community, further information and lesson activity ideas.

- Schooling in different countries – Use the example of Malala Yousafzai's global campaign for education for girls.

- Explore gender equality in different countries. (There is a useful link with mathematics (see 'Mathematics/Numeracy') – if you look at global statistics some countries in the Global South are doing better than the Global North, for example, Rwandan women's representation in parliament.)

- Women in sustainability, for example, Kenyan Nobel Peace Prize Winner, Wangari Maathai (see Appendix 4 for a list of children's books).

- www.divinechocolate.com/divinewomen – Case studies of how women have been centrally involved in a variety of roles in this fair trade chocolate company.

HISTORY

A survey for Girlguiding (2016) of 1600 girls and young women across the UK found that over half of those surveyed (aged 11–21) said that the role women have played in history is not represented as much as the role of men, and only 41 per cent of them said that their school materials represented women equally to men. History provides an important opportunity to learn about the everyday lives of ordinary people in the past as well as those who are well known. Understanding gender relationships in the past gives an important context to how things are today.

Questions and suggestions

- Do you study famous women in history? Examples in the National Curriculum in England KS1 are Mary Seacole, Rosa Parks and Emily Davison.

- Study the role of women during the World Wars when celebrating Remembrance Day.

- Explore the lives of women in ancient history, for example, Rome and Greece (plus Boudica, queen of the British Celtic Iceni tribe who led an uprising against the occupying forces of the Roman Empire, mentioned in the English National Curriculum KS2).

- Study famous men involved in non-stereotyped roles, for example, peace building – Gandhi, Martin Luther King and Nelson Mandela.[2]

- Study girls and women's position in society/gender roles through time (for example, from Victorian, First and Second World Wars, and the decades since then).

- Study the history of feminism from suffragettes until the current time.

Resources

- www.thoughtco.com/womens-history-4133260 – American site with useful reference articles for teachers.

- www.womenshistorymonth.gov/for-teachers – American site with source materials and suggestions for lessons.

- www.english-heritage.org.uk/learn/histories/women-in-history – Selection of biographies of significant women in English history.

- www.historicengland.org.uk/research/inclusive-heritage/womens-history – Resources relating to the history of women's lives in England.

LANGUAGES

The compulsory study of a foreign (ancient or modern) language at KS2 (ages 7–11) was introduced in England in 2014. Currently, in England, girls outperform boys in modern foreign languages (MFL) at GCSE and more girls select MFL at A level.[3] There has been some research and guidance on how to boost boys' motivation in languages in secondary schools (see, for example, Jones 2017), with recognition that this needs to start at primary level. As with English literacy the guidance points towards improving teaching methods generally rather than any specifically boy-friendly approaches which might inadvertently reinforce stereotyping or disadvantage girls.

Questions and suggestions

- When teaching a foreign language ensure there are specific purposes and real audiences.

- Ensure that students understand the relevance to their own lives of learning a language. Make the link with global citizenship and intercultural learning.

- Consider choosing a language that is represented in the school and local community (such as Mandarin, Arabic or Urdu, for example). This can be affirming for English as an additional language speakers, enabling them to be experts in their subject.

- Teach the language as part of learning about a different culture or countries around the world where the language is spoken.

- Ask students what would help them to enjoy learning a foreign language.

- When providing competition make this against 'personal bests' rather than against others. An emphasis on collaborative work rather than the idea of 'winners and losers' has been found to be particularly motivating for less able learners – both boys and girls.

- As with all good teaching practice letting students know the lesson objectives and how specific activities relate to these can help in demystifying language learning and helping students to feel more control over their learning.

- Ensure foreign languages have a high status and visible profile within the school reflected in dual language displays and welcome posters, etc. Make links with first language speakers in the local community.

- Challenge any assumptions students might have that learning French is more for girls.[4]

Resources

- https://schoolsonline.britishcouncil.org/international-learning/languages/teaching-resources – British Council Schools Online resource with guidance and lesson plans.

MATHEMATICS/NUMERACY

Mathematics is one of the STEM subjects which has been extensively documented as having a problematically low participation of girls post-16. Nearly twice as many boys as girls entered A level mathematics in 2012–2103 and with further mathematics there were nearly three times as many boys (Smith 2014). As with English and literacy, good mathematics teaching is crucial as 'active, engaged, meaning-making pedagogies promote learning; encourage the development of authoritative, confident learners; and provide opportunities to increase social justice within mathematics classrooms' (Povey 2017, p.13). Learning about how mathematics has been developed by mathematicians which include women makes mathematics a more accessible discipline. 'Being aware of historical and cultural contexts also opens up consideration of who "owns" mathematics and challenges conventional appropriations with respect to gender and ethnicity' (Povey 2017, p.18).

Questions and suggestions

- Do you ensure that students have access to a wide range of images of people using mathematics in different occupations and roles, and do these include young and old mathematics users, attractive and not attractive, sporty and not sporty? Are users of average ability and career success included?

- Do you give all children the opportunity to learn how mathematics has been developed by mathematicians including women?

- Do you ensure that girls gain experience and skills involving the interpretation of 2D drawings of 3D objects and mental rotation of these images? This is an area where boys are found consistently to excel compared to girls, and it is an important skill for engineering, architecture, geometry, craft or construction work which can be taught and developed through practice, for example, with video games or making 2D plans with 3D objects.

- Do you give girls encouragement and feedback to help overcome any mathematics anxiety owing to stereotype threat (also supporting under-confident boys)?

- Do you allow group discussion and multiple strategies for understanding and problem solving? 'Classrooms that use formative assessment, exploration and discussion, that do not proceed too quickly to assessment and that allow students to master concepts in depth are supportive for girls and boys' (Smith 2014, p.19).

- Do you help families to build 'science capital' by building networks of information for families about the diverse ways in which pupils can use mathematics learnt in school?

Resources

- www.furthermaths.org.uk/girls-careers – Some case studies of women using mathematics in different careers.

- www.mathscareers.org.uk – Information about careers which use mathematics.

- www.mathscareers.org.uk/article/five-famous-female-mathematicians – Short biographies of ancient and modern famous female mathematicians.

- www.stem.org.uk/resources/collection/4372/inspiring-scientists – Case studies of current British scientists with minority ethnic heritage. Each resource has a film of the scientist or mathematician talking about their work and a timeline of their life and a STEM lesson plan for primary and secondary age groups.

- Global statistics on gender equality presented in many different ways. Individual countries can be looked at and countries can be compared with each other.[5]

- In work on Ancient Greece include Hypatia[6] who was the first woman mathematician about whom we have biographical and mathematical information.

- Florence Nightingale's lesser-known contribution was as a statistician.[7]

MUSIC

Although music is one of the few GCSE subjects chosen equally by girls and boys, this doesn't mean that issues to do with gender stereotyping in music don't exist. As with artists, sports people, scientists, historians and mathematicians, classical composers still tend to be thought of as male and White. There may still be gender segregation in a primary school in relation to which musical instruments are chosen and who is involved in the choir. With an increase in the use of music technology for music production there is an increased danger of girls being excluded.

Questions and suggestions

- Is there gender differentiation in who learns which musical instrument in your school, for example, boys learning brass/electric guitar/drums and girls learning strings/woodwind?

- Is singing seen as a normal activity for all genders to participate in? Are boys encouraged to join school choirs? Are many boys' negative attitudes towards singing countered with visits from male singers and male teachers teaching singing or performing?

- Are girls and boys equally involved with different musical styles, for example, boys in the orchestra, girls in rock bands?

- Are there differences in teachers' attitudes to girls' and boys' musical ability and are boys as well as girls expected to record their musical ideas using traditional or graphic notation, etc.?

- In work with percussion do girls and boys get an equal chance to play all the instruments (including the larger drums for girls, and glockenspiel/triangle for boys)?

- Do you ensure that girls as well as boys have access to music technology and the skills to use it?

- Do you and your pupils know as many female classical composers as male?

- Do you play a variety of recorded music from different places, times and involving women and men?

Resources

- www.bbc.co.uk/programmes/p02kn2t6 (Radio 3 Celebrating Women Composers) – This is a rich source of information about historical and contemporary female composers with audio and video clips of music.

PHYSICAL EDUCATION (PE)

Ann-Carita Evaldsson, in her research on gender differences across game contexts, suggests:

> the teacher's orientation towards gender equality/sameness and cross-sex activities and the availability of sports activities for girls outside school…helped the girls with minority and lower working class backgrounds to develop physical skills, challenge boys' domination

and employ power positions in games in the playground. (Evaldsson 2003, p.495)

Questions and suggestions

- Do all girls and boys get equal access to a full range of physical, sporting and games activities?

- Is boys' involvement in dance and gymnastics encouraged?

- Is girls' involvement in football and other ball games encouraged?

- Is there a focus on skills development in PE lessons rather than competition? Is support differentiated to ensure that all children can participate?

- Consider positive and counter-stereotypical gender role models when inviting sports coaches to come in to school from outside organisations – do you ensure they know the gender equality principles of the school?

- Do pupils have the opportunity to learn about famous male dancers/gymnasts, famous female footballers/rugby players, etc.?

- Are teams mixed while ensuring that girls are confident and boys don't dominate? What gendered messages are the school teams sending to other pupils about the possibility of their participation and success?

- Do you provide a variety of sporting and fitness opportunities outside of school – including basketball, climbing, etc.?

Resources

- An internet search will come up with female and male sports and dance role models. For example: https://www.theguardian.com/football/2016/aug/03/the-20-greatest-female-football-players-soccer is a list with photos and short biographies of famous football players from around the world.

- https://balletboard.com/top-11-famous-male-ballet-dancers/ lists famous male ballet dancers from around the world.

PSHE AND CITIZENSHIP

Many of the lesson plans and activities developed by teachers during the Gender Respect Project come under the curriculum heading of PSHE and Citizenship. See Chapter 7 for lesson plans and activities and examples of how children can be involved in participating as citizens in change relating to gender equality.

Questions and suggestions

- Do you help boys to develop a full range of emotional vocabulary and understanding of emotions? Do boys know that it is okay for them to be sensitive and caring and to show sadness as well as anger? Do girls know that they can feel and express a full range of emotions including anger?

- Are issues to do with the influence of social media on body image discussed?

- Are all pupils supported in developing respectful relationships with each other including the meaning of consent from a young age?

- Are all pupils taught that changes such as menstruation at puberty are natural and healthy?

- Consider involving the school council in auditing gender equality in the school and planning for change.

- Are boys and girls equally involved in conflict resolution initiatives such as peer mediation or playground buddies?

- Are all children taught the skills of non-violent conflict resolution and shown examples of men and women from history and globally who were peace makers or involved in non-violent action for change (for example, Wangari Maathai,

Gandhi, Malala, Martin Luther King)? See Appendix 4 for a list of books.

- Do girls know that women are involved in politics across the world?

- Are children aware that equality is enshrined in the International Convention on the Rights of the Child and the Universal Declaration of Human Rights? See Appendix 4 for a list of children's books.

Resources

- www.periodpositive.com – Chella Quint's website with guidance for talking about menstruation, challenging societal taboos and developing media literacy.

- www.bbc.co.uk/cbbc/curations/international-womens-day – History, sport, literature, films and quizzes for children.

- www.genderrespect2013.wordpress.com/teaching-ideas/ one-billion-rising – One Billion Rising (OBR) annual event on 14 February – PowerPoint to introduce OBR and poetry lesson plan.

- www.bbc.co.uk/newsround – Check for gender-related news stories/those which challenge gender stereotypes.

- See www.hindehouseprimary.net/Data/Parent_Downloads/ SexandRelationshipEducation.pdf for an example of a RSE policy from one of the Gender Respect Project schools.

RELIGIOUS EDUCATION (RE)

RE provides an excellent opportunity to discuss ethical issues, including that of gender equality, but it is important that teachers understand the diversity of ways of life and beliefs that exist within each of the major religions so that assumptions can be challenged. When teaching about religious stories, there is a danger of uncritically focusing on key male figures to the exclusion of women. Teachers may have to go out of their way to ensure gender balance.

Questions and suggestions

- Are assumptions made about the role of women in different religions? How can these be explored and challenged?

- Is the role of women across all faiths explored (including Christianity)? Have the roles changed over time? Are religions seen as diverse rather than monolithic? How are different approaches to major faiths explored?

- Are people of diverse backgrounds portrayed in all religions?

- Do you enable students to explore a diverse range of perspectives about gender and religion?

- Are women shown to have played important roles in different religions (for example, judges: Deborah (Judaism); leaders: Rani of Jhansi (Sikhism); prophets: Nehanda of Zimbabwe (Animism, Shona); mystics: Rabia'al Adawiyyah (Sufism/Islam); shamans and visionaries (Animism); saints: St Theresa of Avila (Christianity); courageous and inspirational figures: Sojourner Truth, Mary Seacole (Christianity), etc.; see Hanlon 1992).

- Are women from different faiths invited in to talk about their day-to-day experiences and patterns of life?

- If people from faith traditions are invited in to lead assemblies, what messages about gender equality do they give? Are women invited in as much as men?

Resources

- Invite people of different faiths in to school to talk about their religion, using resources such as BBC Bitesize class clips: www.bbc.co.uk/education/topics/zpdtsbk/resources/2, in particular *The Hijaab*, where one girl explains why she decided to wear the Hijaab.

- A photo slide show of contemporary female religious leaders of many different faiths from all over the world – https://www.huffingtonpost.com/2014/03/08/women-religious-leaders_n_4922118.html?slideshow=true#gallery/340343/14.

- Useful background reading for teachers: 'Debunking myths on Women's Rights, Muslim Women, Feminism and Islamophobia in Europe' by the European Network Against Racism – http://www.enar-eu.org/IMG/pdf/debunkingmyths_lr_final.pdf.

SCIENCE

A now well-known statistic is that the proportion of female A level physics students has remained at around 20 per cent for the last 20 years or so. Girls are more likely to study biology:

> which is commonly seen as the 'easiest' science, playing into gender stereotypes about the intellectual capacity of girls for STEM. These careers are also more likely to be linked in wider consciousness to value-based careers decisions like wanting to 'help people' and 'change the world'. (Zecharia *et al*. 2014, p.16)

It is essential that all aspects of science are made interesting and accessible to girls in primary schools.

Questions and suggestions

- Do you show the diversity of possible careers involving science, challenging gender stereotypes?

- Do you actively encourage boys' interest in topics relating to biology and girls' interest in those relating to physics (for example, space)?

- As a teacher do you model interest in non-gender-stereotyped areas of science?

- Do you have the knowledge and confidence in science that you need to support children's attainment and progression?

- Do you actively portray female scientists as well as male?

Resources

- www.amightygirl.com/blog?p=11511 – 'Those Who Dared To Discover: 16 Women Scientists You Should Know'.

- www.stem.org.uk/resources/collection/4372/inspiring-scientists – Case studies of current British scientists with minority ethnic heritage. Each resource has a film of the scientist talking about their work and a timeline of their life and a STEM lesson plan for primary and secondary age groups. Five out of the ten scientists featured are women.

SUMMARY

This chapter has:

- – provided some questions and guidance for embedding gender equality into the different subject areas in the primary curriculum.

Chapter 7

EXPLICIT TEACHING

In the previous two chapters I have offered some guidance on how to promote gender equality in the hidden curriculum and integrate it into subject areas in a primary school. Although these form an essential backdrop, extensive research has found that such approaches alone are not sufficient to really challenge children's ideas about gender roles and behaviours. Rather than passively receive the influences around them, children actively construct meaning and so need to be supported in critically evaluating the ideas about gender which they are subject to on a day-to-day basis. In the Early Years, for example, it is not enough to provide an environment where alternative role models are available (in the form of staffing, images, stories, etc.) in the hope that the children will soak these up and that they will provide a counterpoint to the compelling evidence of how to perform masculinities and femininities provided by the world at large as well as their peers. Active intervention is needed to support children in their 'border work' of non-stereotypical play; challenging sexist comments or dominating behaviour; extending their play storylines; and providing ongoing opportunities for children to discuss with each other how they understand and feel about gender, what is fair and unfair in their day-to-day relationships with each other and so on.

Stephen, a nursery teacher recounts an intervention he made:

'Today was the first day that I noticed two boys in nursery openly challenging girls who tried to join in. The first case was at the construction area outside. I was actively supporting children in trying areas not in use. I entered the construction area and one of the boys followed. We started to move bricks, level with a spirit level and measure. One of the girls moved to the area and asked the boy whether she could join us. "No" she was told. I challenged with, "Why not?"

"Building is for big men," was the reply, "you have big men and boys not girls."

I challenged with, "Girls build as well as boys."

"No they don't. I told you, it's big men and boys," the boy said.

I challenged again with, "What makes girls different from boys to stop them?"

I then supported understanding with a conversation that highlighted that girls could do the same as boys. The girl returned and her friend joined in. The boy accepted the girls as I had challenged him but I'm not convinced he would have let them without my presence.

Then later, children were in the middle of role-play, supporting fantasy with wooden block play. "Let's go to our boys' castle," one of the boys called.

"Just boys?" I challenged, "Why just boys? Why not girls?"

"The castle is for superheroes and you can't have girl super-heroes."

I named a handful.

"They have Cat Woman but she is bad. She is not a superhero," was the answer.

I then named similar villains who were boys. I could see he was reflecting on his thoughts through being challenged. He was persuaded to let the girls enter the castle.'

As children move through primary school, direct intervention is recommended to ameliorate gender stereotypes that already exist. Research has shown that 'in the absence of direct interventions children with highly stereotyped attitudes are likely to distort incoming counter-stereotypical information to make it stereotype consistent thus reinforcing rather than reducing stereotype' (Liben *et al.* 2001, p.358). This has been found in relation to non-stereotyped television content (Durkin 1985) and with the use of counter-stereotypical picture books. Skelton and Francis (2003) give an account of Bronwyn Davies' research 'Frogs and Snails and Feminist Tales' (2002) where alternative fairy tales were read to young children but they were unable to hear the intended message of the stories as it didn't fit with their own ideas of gender categories. For example, in the case of *The Paper Bag Princess* (Munsch and Martchenko 1980), where Elizabeth, the princess, rescues prince Ronald from the dragon who burns her dress so she has to wear a paper bag, the children hearing this story rejected Elizabeth as being deviant and empathised with Ronald who disapproved of Elizabeth not looking pretty any more. As Skelton and Francis point out:

> It is not enough to simply expose children to feminist texts, nor is it enough to ask them to interpret those texts on the basis of their experiences…they need as well to discover themselves in the act of sense making, of importing their own knowledges into the text (and of importing ideas and images from the text into their lived storylines) in order to examine the complex relations between lived experience and text. They need to discover the ways in which their category memberships (as male or female, white or black) lead them to interpret differently and to be positioned differently in the text…the authority of the author needs to be disrupted. (Skelton and Francis 2003, p.138)

PHILOSOPHY FOR CHILDREN (P4C)

One example of such a 'direct intervention' is the use of Philosophy for Children (P4C).[1] P4C is a dialogic learning approach which was used successfully in the Gender Respect Project to engage children in questioning their assumptions, sharing alternative perspectives, challenging each other and examining the validity of their reasons for a particular view. During the Gender Respect Project scoping study the process of articulating their own reasons and hearing others' reasons led in some cases to students experienced in P4C changing their mind about their views. One nine-year-old boy, who had previously said in response to a photograph of a female electrician up a stepladder, 'Girls aren't as strong as boys and a girl might get an electric shock…and just fall down', having listened to another student's explanation of why he didn't like the picture of a woman builder 'because how can a woman hold a heavy thing while climbing a ladder…cos she might fall off', argued, 'It's not like a boy wouldn't fall off. I'm going upstairs and I'm like a man and a girl's coming upstairs with a heavy thing and she comes up and I fall down. It doesn't mean you've got super powers if you're a man.'

P4C aims to develop a community of philosophical enquiry where children and young people engage in communal dialogue to find answers to questions about life that they find compelling. These questions are philosophical in nature but are not confined to any one curriculum or subject area. With children these questions may be described as 'big' or 'chewy' and they explore central concepts such as right and wrong, rights and responsibilities, how we know about things and what we appreciate and value as human beings. These correspond with some of the traditional branches of philosophy: ethics, politics, epistemology and aesthetics.

A community of philosophical enquiry operates well when four kinds of thinking are engaged: critical thinking, creative thinking, caring thinking and collaborative thinking. These have come to be known in P4C as the 'Four Cs' of thinking and all four are seen to have equal importance. This is one of the characteristics of P4C that makes it a unique pedagogy: it recognises that for good thinking the intellectual and affective need to work together.

Central to P4C is the idea of 'reasonableness'. A 'reasonable' person is someone who is able to think logically, question ideas and make distinctions and connections (intellectual skills) but is also willing to listen to the perspectives of others and modify their own thinking in light of these. A 'reasonable' person also has the skill to recognise the consequences of their thinking on their own lives and the disposition to change their behaviour accordingly.

CRITICAL THINKING

In P4C children develop the skills to critically engage with the information and viewpoints that they encounter in their lives, and to be able to recognise and challenge bias, indoctrination and propaganda.

They learn to identify and question assumptions and consider how context influences meaning. They think about the likely consequences of actions and learn to make judgements and decisions based on good reasons. P4C involves a process of opening out or problematising an issue or concept. Through critical enquiry, understanding about gender roles and relationships can be clarified and deepened. Alongside this critical engagement, P4C encourages openness to other people's ideas and perspectives and a willingness to change opinions in the face of new evidence and rational arguments.

CREATIVE THINKING

Philosophical enquiry gives children the chance to wonder, speculate and try out their tentative ideas. They are encouraged to look at problems in different ways and to imagine alternative possibilities.

CARING THINKING

Research on P4C carried out with young children by a clinical psychologist, Elizabeth Doherr (2000), uncovered the success of P4C in helping children to name different emotions and make links between thoughts and feelings. This in itself will support children in developing emotional literacy skills, which has been shown to be particularly important for boys to counteract the burden of societal expectations to be 'tough'.

The opportunity, within a community of enquiry, to deeply listen allows children to put themselves in another's shoes, to empathise and potentially understand.

The notion of 'caring thinking', originated by Matthew Lipman and further developed by his colleague Ann Sharpe, encapsulates this bringing together of the emotions and intellect. 'Caring thinking' is not just the procedural aspects of respect and listening to others required for a community of enquiry to function, caring about *someone*, but also crucially encompasses caring about *something*. In P4C children make up their own questions and choose the one that they think is most important. They then engage in a discussion about that important matter and even learn 'that there are some things that you can think deeply about' (quote from a ten-year-old child who had participated in P4C for several years).

COLLABORATIVE THINKING

A community of enquiry is by its very nature collaborative. P4C provides a real context for collaboration in which children work together to seek answers to a question and grapple with ideas. It is only through listening and working together that the goal of trying to find answers to a question or deeper understanding of a concept can be achieved.

STEPS IN AN ENQUIRY

P4C provides a ten-step framework within which the community of philosophical enquiry can develop. This framework is designed to take up a traditional lesson length of about an hour, but can be adapted to take up a shorter time for very young children or spread over two or more lessons for older children. As a group of students and the teacher become familiar with the process, the steps can then be used more flexibly according to the needs of a particular enquiry, group of students or the curriculum. For example, the stimulus for an enquiry may arise out of some work in a particular curriculum area or a new enquiry may start where a previous enquiry left off, with a summary of key ideas discussed and a decision-making process to choose what to focus on. An enquiry may throw up some questions suitable for research and this could be conducted by the students between enquiries. There may be specific skills-focused work that it would be fruitful to concentrate on (for example, work on developing questioning skills) or time might usefully be spent on exercises to explore concepts that have arisen during an enquiry or appear in a question prior to its discussion.

1. Getting set

- Students seated in a circle or horseshoe shape to enable dialogue between them.

- Rules for P4C developed with students (relating to listening, respect, etc.).

- Game or activity which either develops enquiry skills or relates to the content of the stimulus.

2. Presentation of stimulus

- A starting point which provokes questions and can be returned to as a shared context during the discussion.

- Stimulus could be a picture book or story, other text fiction or non-fiction; other narrative such as film or animation; music, pictures or objects; or a combination of different media. In the lesson plans that follow there are examples of different resources that can be used as stimuli to provoke discussion about gender equality.

- Needs to be something which is thought-provoking for the group, something which will make them want to ask questions.

3. Thinking time (about the stimulus)

- Time to reflect on the stimulus.

- Thinking time is essential and should be built into the enquiry whenever it is appropriate.

- Could be timed (for example, with a minute timer) individual thinking.

- Ask students, 'What are you wondering?' 'What interests you about the stimulus?'

- Students could talk in pairs and feed back a summary or one word to capture their ideas.

- Students could write in their 'Philosophy jotters' (individual notebooks for children to use during and after P4C).

4. Question formulation

- Important that students develop their own questions rather than being given a question by the teacher, so that the children feel engaged and have ownership of the enquiry. Asking questions is a critical and creative process important to learning.

- With a group new to P4C or younger children this could be done as a whole group – gather thoughts and questions and write them down on a flipchart or whiteboard – point out when a question is given but don't show bias towards any one idea or question.

- Questions could be developed by the students in pairs or small groups. You could say: 'Think of a question which you are really interested in talking about and one which we can find some answers together by talking and thinking without needing to look things up on the internet or asking the author/director (if the stimulus is a book/film).'

- Teachers describe such questions as 'big', 'chewy', 'about life', 'deep and meaningful', 'philosophical'.

- Write questions on a whiteboard, flipchart or individual pieces of paper (but large enough for everyone to see).

5. Question airing

- All questions are understood and valued.

- Students explain how they came up with the question and how it relates to the stimulus.

- Could make connections/distinctions between questions.

- Could identify assumptions in the question.

- Students could ask for clarification or elaboration of others' questions.

- A more experienced community could sort questions into 'research' or 'reflection' and then choose from the 'reflection' questions and use the 'research' questions in other lessons. An example of two such questions relating to gender equality might be: Research: 'How many nurses are male?' Reflection: 'Is it important for all genders to be able to do all occupations?'

6. Question selecting

- Needs to be fair.

- Omni-votes (can vote for all) or multi-vote (for example, two or three votes) or preferential voting or random selection?

- Secret (for example, outward-facing circle with thumbs up behind back to vote) or open ballot (for example, put counters on questions or stand near question)?

7. First thoughts (about the question chosen)

- Could go round to find out everyone's initial ideas (could restrict to two or three words). Anyone can pass.

- Could share first thoughts in pairs or ask students who made up the question chosen to start the discussion off.

8. Building

- Consider how students will take turns speaking, for example, put hand out when person who is talking has finished then teacher chooses next person or last speaker chooses (but teacher has right to intervene at any time to facilitate enquiry) or 'speak into the space' where students just wait for an opportunity to speak when no one else is speaking (an important skill for anyone to learn in group discussion).

- Consider using different hand signals when children are more experienced, for example, thumb up for new point or fists on top of each other for building on someone else's idea. This supports children's metacognition or ability to think about their thinking as well as helping the enquiry to build.

- Consider your role as facilitator (see 'Facilitating P4C – The Role of the Teacher').

9. Last thoughts

- Chance for final words uncontested (often students who haven't spoken in the large group before use this opportunity to contribute).

- Back to pair discussion or go round with 'talking object' (can only speak when holding object). One turn each.

- Could ask, 'How far have we got with trying to find answers to the question?' or 'What are the implications of what we have been talking about for your lives?'

10. Review

- Chance for students to reflect on process of enquiry using, for example, two stars and a wish, plus, minus, interesting or www/ebi (what went well/even better if) or a quick visual feedback, for example, thumbs up if you enjoyed the discussion/learnt something new/changed your mind.

- More in-depth review could be done once a term in a separate lesson.

- Important that review doesn't become an opportunity to assess 'performance' of the group. Evaluation needs to be formative and focused on having better discussions.

- Review could look at whether there are there any themes/issues that the group would like to follow up (either in private research, in another lesson or in a future enquiry).

FACILITATING P4C – THE ROLE OF THE TEACHER

Facilitating P4C is both hugely enjoyable and challenging for most teachers. It is thus duly accorded a substantial amount of time on the SAPERE[2] Level 1 and 2 training courses[3] and therefore can only briefly be touched upon here. Even teachers accustomed to enquiry-based learning often find it challenging to let go of the reins in P4C and give over control of the learning to the students, especially during the 'building' part of the enquiry. It is important that the group is engaged in genuine dialogue with each other rather than with the teacher, that the students are, in fact, thinking for themselves rather than second-guessing what is in the teacher's head. To enable this to happen it is recommended that the facilitator refrains from offering their own point of view and makes substantive interventions only in the form of tentative, open questions (in the sense that there is more than one possible answer) that support the students' thinking in response to what they have said – for example, 'Do you have to be a "sporty girl" or a "girly girl" or fit into some other group? Do people need groups to belong to? How much freedom does belonging to a group give you?' Other interventions will be procedural and concerned with supporting the 'Four Cs' of thinking (see above). The facilitator might ask for a reason or an example, a summary or a different point; they may scaffold the students in their turn taking or listening or respect for each other; they always act in response to what the students are saying or doing. Facilitation requires curiosity and deep and attentive listening to what the students are actually saying, with focused concentration to follow closely the threads of the children's thinking. The facilitator keeps track of the progress of the enquiry for the group, enabling them to revisit earlier points if they become relevant and helping them to notice if the discussion takes a different direction. The facilitator will be continually evaluating when and how to make an intervention to challenge the children's thinking and support the progress of the enquiry and when to hold back.

CONCEPTS RELATING TO GENDER THAT COULD BE EXPLORED IN P4C

Gender, Equality, Equity, Human Rights, Beauty, Freedom, Choice, Stereotyping, Fairness, Justice, Identity, Belonging, Respect, Democracy, Talents, Skills, Learning, Appearance, Power and Friendship

---

Question plans

These are lists of questions which might be useful for a facilitator to ask during an enquiry to push children's thinking further. Ideally the facilitator should prepare an enquiry with their own questions based on the concepts in the philosophical question generated and chosen by the children. The questions are for guidance only and should be used only if they would help children with their enquiry, and only after listening carefully to what the children are saying (rather than randomly popping them in). It is usually more powerful if the children can challenge each other's thinking, so careful consideration needs to be given before asking such questions as a facilitator.

Example question plans

APPEARANCE

Is looking after your appearance a waste of time?

Should you always care about your appearance?

When is it important to care about your appearance?

Should some people care about their appearance more than others? What about actors/air stewards/doctors?

Is it more important to care about your appearance if you are a girl/boy?

Are girls judged more by their appearance than boys?

Should you be able to wear what you like?

Who decides what people should wear?

Who decides what people should look like?

Why do people dress boy babies in blue and girl babies in pink?

Would it matter if you couldn't tell the difference between girls and boys just by looking at them?

Can you judge a book by its cover?

BEAUTY

Is it important to be beautiful?

Could being beautiful ever be a bad thing?

Is it more important for girls to be beautiful than for boys to be beautiful?

Are princesses always beautiful? Are witches always ugly? Why?

Should boys wear make-up?

Are old people beautiful?

Who decides who is beautiful?

Can someone with an ugly face be beautiful?

Just because the media say that someone is beautiful, are they?

Does beauty give you power?

POWER

When have you felt powerful?

What makes people powerful?

Can you be powerful and kind at the same time?

Can women be more powerful than men?

Should everyone have equal power?

How do people use power?

If you are a powerful person are you always powerful in every situation?

Does power give people freedom?

Does power mean you have responsibility?

GENDER ROLES/STEREOTYPING

Are men better at some jobs than women? Are women better at some jobs than men?

Is there such a thing as boys' toys and girls' tovys?

Should boys and girls play with different things?

Does what you play with when you're little influence what you can do when you're older? Does what you play with when you're a child influence what you are interested in when you're older?

Is it just some girls/boys that like boys'/girls' things? Why?

What are boys'/girls' things?

Should everybody like everything?

Should it matter whether you are a girl or a boy?

Can anybody choose to like anything?

Can anybody choose to do anything?

What about boys choosing to dress up in princess outfits?

Are girls and boys different?

FRIENDSHIP

Can girls and boys be friends with each other?

Does this change depending on how old you are?

Should girls and boys be friends with each other?

Should girls and boys be able to be friends with each other?

Can a girl have a best friend who is a boy?

Can a boy have a best friend who is girl?

Do girls understand boys?

Do boys understand girls?

If you play with a girl/boy does that mean that you fancy them/are going out with them?

What if you don't see yourself as a boy or a girl, can you be friends with anybody?

Does gender matter in friendship?

FAIRNESS

If you're better than someone else at a job should you always be the one to do it?

Does fairness mean everyone being equal? (Fairness and equality)

Does fairness mean everyone being treated the same way?

Should all members of a family share housework? (Stereotyping and fairness)

How would you decide if something is unfair?

EQUALITY

Should everybody be equal?

Does being equal mean being the same?

Should everyone get the same amount of help to do their mathematics?

Should everyone get the same results in a test?

Do some people need more help than others?

Should there always be a boy and girl prefect/member of school council, etc.?

Should everybody get the same amount of time to speak in class?

FREEDOM

Do boys have more freedom than girls?

What is it that makes you free or unfree?

Does freedom give you power? (Freedom and power)

Are beautiful people more or less free? (Freedom and beauty)

Can anybody choose to like anything?

Can anybody choose to do anything?

Are we free when we can be ourselves?

Is it possible to be free when other people are not free?

IDENTITY/BELONGING

How important is your gender to who you are?

Is gender an important part of who you are?

Is it possible to be a girl and a boy at the same time?

How do people know which gender they are?

Could we have a world without gender? What would that be like?

Do you have to be a 'sporty girl' or a 'girly girl' or fit into a certain group?

Do people need groups to belong to?

When is it helpful to belong to a group?

When is belonging to a group unhelpful? Does being in a group give you more freedom or less freedom? (Belonging and freedom)

TALENTS AND SKILLS

Is it possible to learn how to do anything?

Are there some things that girls/boys are better at? If so, why?

Are boys only better at football because they've practised it a lot?

Are girls naturally better at talking about their feelings?

Are all things learnt or are you born with some talents?

How different are girls' and boys' skills and talents?

Are women better than men at looking after babies? How do you know?

What would make men better at looking after babies?

Can you get better at anything with practice?

The lesson plans that follow have been developed and used by teachers on the Gender Respect Project. P4C is used at various points to engage children critically in discussion about gender issues.

LESSON PLANS

- Thinking about gender roles

- Gender and work

- Gender and sport

- Identity, body image and relationships

- Violence and prejudice

- Senses poetry workshop

THINKING ABOUT GENDER ROLES

ACTIVITY 1: THINKING ABOUT GENDER ROLES

Summary/purpose: This lesson, aimed at students aged 7–11, requires students to consider various gender identities and roles. Using the framework of a Venn diagram, students are asked to separate adjectives, jobs, domestic duties and childcare responsibilities into men, women or both sets. Students should then think critically about their choices and reflect on different scenarios.

Curriculum links: PSHE, Citizenship, English

Resources: Venn diagrams printed onto A3 sheets with overlapping circles, one per group (a template is available to download from www.jkp.com/catalogue/book/9781785923401); Word-sort sets cut up and placed into envelopes (Table 7.1).

Procedure:

1. Choose one of the four word-sort activities: (a) Adjectives; (b) Jobs; (c) Domestic roles; (d) Childcare.

2. Ask students in pairs or small groups to place the words/ statements on the Venn diagram according to whether they

perceive the word/statement to be associated with men, women or both men and women.

3. How did they decide? What sort of discussion was there? Where do their ideas about how to decide come from? (N.B. with domestic roles and childcare they are very likely to be influenced by what happens in their family, so there will be issues if, for example, there are single parents. What if, for example, one of the parents goes out to work or both go out to work?)

4. Would their answers look different if the activity was done:

   a. at the time their grandparents were children? (Or 60 years ago?)

   b. at the time their parents were children? (Or 25 years ago?)

   c. by a child in 20 years' time (in the future)?

5. What has this activity taught the students about gender roles? How are the roles of men and women changing? How would they like them to be?

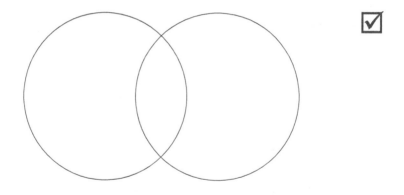

Figure 7.1 Venn diagram

Table 7.1 Thinking about gender roles

a) Adjectives	
Strong	Weak
Caring	Uncaring
Kind	Mean
Noisy	Quiet

cont.

a) Adjectives	
Tough	Gentle
Brave	Timid
Friendly	Unfriendly
Thoughtful	Sensitive
Shy	Tidy
b) Jobs	
Nurse	Doctor
Surgeon	Firefighter
Teacher	Pilot
Headteacher	CEO / Manager
Soldier	Scientist
Inventor	Carer
Footballer	Dancer
Artist	Social worker
c) Domestic roles	
Cooking	Cleaning
Gardening	Paying the bills
Washing up	Ironing clothes
Looking after the car	Fixing a computer problem
Fixing things in the home (DIY)	Painting and decorating
Chopping wood	Choosing holidays
Doing the shopping	Earning money
Washing clothes	Emptying bins
Sewing	Making the beds
d) Childcare	
Changing nappies	Taking to school
Helping with homework	Going to parents' evening
Giving lifts in the car	Washing and ironing clothes
Taking to dentist or doctor	Food shopping
Reading stories	Going to sports events
Buying clothes	Giving a cuddle
Giving punishment	Giving a bath
Preparing meals	Going to playgrounds

ACTIVITY 2: GENDER ROLES –
ASSUMPTIONS AND FAIRNESS

Summary: This lesson is based on a workshop delivered by the Gender Respect Project annually at the CRESST (Conflict Resolution in Education Sheffield Schools Training) Peer Mediators' Conference, where primary-aged peer mediators from all over Sheffield gather together to have fun and learn more about conflict. It uses the set of images from the scoping study (described in Appendix 1) to provoke discussion and challenge assumptions about gender roles.

Curriculum links: PSHE, English

Resources: Set of A4 images depicting non-stereotyped work and sport and emotions. Flipchart or whiteboard to write notes. Space large enough for students to walk around pictures and move into agree–disagree lines.

Procedure:

SPORT AND PE

Students walk around the sporting images that are on the floor and go to the one that most interests them. Ask each group what they think the image shows and why they chose it. Draw out the attitude or assumption behind their choice.

If one of the students says something which the others find challenging or thought-provoking, use this statement for an agree–disagree line. Otherwise use one of the following statements:

- Boys are better at PE than girls.
- Boys enjoy PE more than girls.
- Girls are better at dance than boys.
- Boys are better at football than girls.

Ask students to stand on the continuum line to show that they agree/disagree/are somewhere in between. Ask students why they are standing there. Draw out attitudes or assumptions and record them on the flipchart.

CAREERS

Students look at the images of different careers displayed on the floor and choose to stand by one that they like/dislike/find interesting and discuss as a group why they have chosen this image.

Ask each group why they chose the image, what they think it shows and if they agree with it.

Draw out attitudes or assumptions and record them on the flip-chart.

Alternative activity:

Ask students to stand on the continuum line to show that they agree/disagree/are somewhere in between regarding the following statements. Ask students why they are standing there.

- Only women should do the cooking and cleaning.

- Men should earn more money than women.

- Women are not capable of being builders.

EMOTIONS

Students look at the images on the floor of men and women showing different emotions. They choose to stand by one that they like/dislike/makes them feel uncomfortable. Ask students to explain why and draw out any stereotypes (such as men don't cry, women don't shout).

REFLECTION

Children get into groups of four or five and discuss the following questions, recording their answers on flipchart paper:

- If you had super magical powers and could make things fairer and kinder between men and women, girls and boys, what one thing would you do?

- As a peer mediator (or other role in school), what could you do to make things fairer?

ACTIVITY 3: WE ARE ONE – WE ARE EQUAL

Summary: This series of six lessons, aimed at students aged 9–11, uses various resources including films, books and information about different countries to explore gender roles and stereotyping in a local-global context.

Curriculum links: English, P4C, Mathematics

LESSON 1: INTRODUCTION OF GENDER ISSUES

Purpose: To start discussing stereotypes and gender equality.

Resources: Sets of stereotypical/gender-equal statements (Table 7.2) – enough for all students to use in pairs.

Procedure:

1. Using the statements (Table 7.2), ask students to pair up and decide whether they agree, disagree or are unsure.

2. Document this by taking photographs of the placement of the statements and discuss views in larger groups. Think carefully about the groups and adjust the number of statements accordingly.

Table 7.2 Stereotypical/gender-equal statements

All children with short hair are boys	Girls should not play football	Girls should not study science at university
Only women should do the cooking and cleaning	Women should not be bus drivers	Boys do not like dancing
Men should not be hairdressers	Men should earn more than women	Boys are stronger than girls
Girls are more intelligent than boys	It is okay for boys to wear pink and girls to wear blue	Alex, Jordan and Ashley are names for both boys and girls
Both men and women should take on roles in the emergency services	All women should have children	Only men should be prime minister
Women are not capable of being builders	It is only okay to buy women flowers	Only men can do DIY
Boys should not play netball		

LESSON 2: P4C ENQUIRY

Purpose: To use P4C to help students think about sexism and stereotyping.

Resources: *Piggybook* by Anthony Browne (1986; see Appendix 4 for more information about this book).

Procedure:
Use the picture book, *Piggybook*, as a stimulus: using the text and illustrations, discuss the book's content before choosing words that really capture the story. Looking at these words, agree on an interesting philosophical question to discuss.

The following ideas may help the discussion:

- What are things like in your house?

- What would you like things to be like?

Don't make any assumptions about the make-up of the children's families – it might be useful to mention that families are all different when initially discussing the book (for example, some families have two mums or two dads or one parent; some children live with grandparents, step parents or foster parents, etc.).

> In the session led by project teacher, Ivonne, many children mentioned how dads, due to work pressures, were not able to spend a lot of time with their children, which made both the dads and the children sad. They also talked about dads enjoying cooking and helping at home, and pointed out that each family is different.

LESSON 3: HUMAN RIGHTS

Purpose: To introduce human rights and equality as a fundamental human right.

Resources: UNICEF Wants and Needs Cards,[4] *We Are All Born Free* picture book (Amnesty International 2008).

Procedure:

Introduce the idea of 'wants' and 'needs' by sorting the cards developed by UNICEF (Decent shelter, Nutritious food, Protection from abuse and neglect, Education, Health care, Fair treatment and non-discrimination, Clean air, Opportunities to share opinions, Playgrounds and recreation, Clean water, Opportunities to practise your own culture, language and religion, Clothes in the latest style, A bicycle, Holiday trips, Your own bedroom, A personal computer, A television set, A mobile phone, Money to spend as you like, Fast food).

In groups, children choose a Needs Card and 'freeze frame' the idea (use their bodies to present a still picture). Other children question those in the frame: 'What are you feeling?' 'What are you doing/thinking?'

Use the picture of 'Right to equality' from *We Are All Born Free* as a stimulus for a P4C enquiry. The picture shows giant scales with boys on one side and girls on the other. During the review of the enquiry, using thought bubbles, consider 'How does gender stereotyping and gender inequality impact on the students themselves within the variety of contexts in which they find themselves (friendships, class, school, home, family)?'

LESSON 4: GENDER INEQUALITY IN ANOTHER COUNTRY

Purpose: To study an example of gender inequality in another country.

Resources: Film of *Wadjda*,[5] writing frame.

Procedure:
This film, which is the first one made by a female director, Haifaa al-Mansour, in Saudi Arabia, tells the story of a girl who is desperate to ride a bicycle. Take two afternoons to watch this, stopping the film to check understanding and discuss in pairs what the issues are around lack of equality. You may want to use your own writing frame to scaffold the children's responses to Wadjda, or discuss the following questions:

- In what ways are girls and boys treated differently in the film?

- What are the similarities and differences with your own context?

LESSON 5: GENDER STEREOTYPING AND GENDER INEQUALITY IN CAREERS

Purpose: To think about gender stereotyping in careers in more depth.

Resources: Visitors, photographs of people in non-stereotypical professions, job descriptions on PowerPoint slides (see below).

Procedure:
If possible try and arrange a visit from a male nurse/male full-time parent/female engineer/female builder. Students will then play 'Twenty questions' to find out what the visitor's job is. Alternatively, photographs can be used or an adult could role-play different professions.

Another activity which works well is to put job descriptions up on PowerPoint slides, asking students to guess the job and who might do it (see below).

Ask questions about the advantages and disadvantages of any of these jobs.

JOB DESCRIPTIONS

Pilot
I work long hours.
I work all over the world.
Safety is my priority.
I take people on holiday.

Hairdresser
I work through the week, as well as some weekends.
I work with the general public.
My job requires good hand-eye coordination.
I shape, colour, cut and curl.

Nurse
I work days and nights.
I am always busy.
I provide hands-on care.
I assist doctors.

Gardener
I work outdoors.

Some may say I have green fingers.
I am very passionate about nature and the environment.
I am very creative.

Police officer
I work closely with members of the public.
I wear a compulsory uniform.
I patrol the streets on foot, by car and by bicycle.
I serve to maintain law and order.

Librarian
My work environment is very quiet.
I work alongside a wealth of resources.
I like to be organised.
The general public like to visit my place of work.

Cook/Chef
I work in a hot and high-pressured environment.
I work as part of a team.
I use a variety of utensils and equipment.
I work with food.

LESSON 6: GLOBAL COMPARISONS ON GENDER INEQUALITY

Purpose: To compare statistics on gender equality in different countries.

Resources: Country statistics (Table 7.3) cut up into separate countries.

Procedure:
Choose one section (see Table 7.3) of gender equality facts (for example, maternity and paternity leave).

In groups or pairs (depending on class size/ability), ask students to discuss the statistics presented on one of the following countries: Rwanda, India, Canada, Cuba, UK and Norway. Share out the different countries between the different groups.

Is there anything they find interesting or surprising? Ask the students as a class to pick the top three countries in terms of equality, awarding them a gold, silver or bronze medal. Continue for each of the other sets of statistics.

Discuss what we could learn from the top three countries in each area.

Table 7.3 Country statistics

Maternity and paternity leave	
Rwanda	The law states that both mothers and fathers are entitled to maternity and paternity leave. Mothers are given 84 days off work at full pay. Fathers are given four days off work at full pay.
India	The law states that only mothers are entitled to maternity leave. Mothers are given 84 days off work at full pay.
Canada	The law states that only mothers are entitled to maternity leave. Mothers are given 105 days off work at full pay.
Cuba	The law states that either a mother or father is entitled to parental leave. Whoever takes parental leave is given 126 days off work at full pay.
UK	The law states that both mothers and fathers are entitled to maternity and paternity leave. Mothers are given 273 days off work at full pay. Fathers are given 14 days off work at full pay.
Norway	There is no law that states that mothers and fathers should receive maternity and paternity leave. However, employers usually agree to parental leave. Whoever takes parental leave is given 343 days off work at full pay.
Pay	
Rwanda	Men and women do not receive the same pay for the same work.
India	Men and women do not receive the same pay for the same work.
Canada	The law states that both men and women should receive the same pay for the same work.
Cuba	The law states that both men and women should receive the same pay for the same work.
UK	The law states that both men and women should receive the same pay for the same work.
Norway	The law states that both men and women should receive the same pay for the same work.
Labour force	
Rwanda	2.6% of the female labour force are currently unemployed compared to 2.4% male.
India	3.8% of the female labour force are currently unemployed compared to 3.3% male.
Canada	6.4% of the female labour force are currently unemployed compared to 7.6% male.

Cuba	3.4% of the female labour force are currently unemployed compared to 2.6% male.
UK	4.6% of the female labour force are currently unemployed compared to 5.1% male.
Norway	4.5% of the female labour force are currently unemployed compared to 5.1% male.
House ownership	
Rwanda	Both married men and women have the right to own a house. This has been law since 1999.
India	Both married men and women have the right to own a house. This has been law since 1874.
Canada	Both married men and women have the right to own a house. This has been law since 1884.
Cuba	Both married men and women have the right to own a house. This has been law since 1917.
UK	Both married men and women have the right to own a house. This has been law since 1822.
Norway	Both married men and women have the right to own a house. This has been law since 1888.
Parliamentarians	
Rwanda	64% of national parliamentarians are women.
India	12% of national parliamentarians are women.
Canada	26% of national parliamentarians are women.
Cuba	49% of national parliamentarians are women.
UK	30% of national parliamentarians are women.
Norway	40% of national parliamentarians are women.
School	
Rwanda	67% of girls and 70% of boys progress from primary to secondary school.
India	91% of girls and 91% of boys progress from primary to secondary school.
Canada	100% of girls and 100% of boys progress from primary to secondary school.
Cuba	99% of girls and 98% of boys progress from primary to secondary school.
UK	100% of girls and 100% of boys progress from primary to secondary school.
Norway	100% of girls and 100% of boys progress from primary to secondary school.

EVALUATION

What have we learnt from the series of lessons? Is there anything we could do to let others in our school/community/country/world know?

P4C ENQUIRY WITH IMAGES FROM THE INTERNET AS A STIMULUS

In a Year 4 (students aged 8–9) enquiry some pictures from an image search for 'gender stereotypes' led to the children's question: 'Why do people think that there are things just for girls and just for boys?'

Here are some of the comments the children made:

On Barbie dolls:
'If you saw a Barbie, a sister might not want to play but a brother might. If a boy wanted something girly, they might want Barbie.'

'Boys might like Barbie but others might laugh.'

'Why should boys like Barbie? That's for girls!'

'Barbie is not just for girls, just because they have long hair and dresses. You can get boy ones too.'

On pink and blue:
'Dolls have pink accessories and packaging. Blue is for boys. I think more girls like pink.'

'Girls and boys are treated differently. Girls like pink and boys like blue. I don't want pink frilly clothes; it's hard when I go shopping.'

'A boy's favourite colour can be purple/pink. A girl's favourite colour can be blue, etc.'

'I used to have a friend who wore a pink frilly dress and her brother wore a dress and a wand. My friend went to a girls' dance school but her brother wasn't allowed to go.'

Toys in general:
'Boys and girls should be treated the same. I don't think it makes any difference if boys and girls like different toys. They should have what they want.'

'Boys might not want a cricket set, but a sporty girl might.'

'Girls might like playing with an Xbox. My brother sometimes plays girls' games.'

'If you went to a toy shop and you wanted a football, it wouldn't be fair if Dad said no.'

'I like parcours. I wanted a bike for my birthday, but I didn't want a "girly" one with hearts and kisses. Boys' bikes are much better.'

'When you go into Tescos, I don't think girls' and boys' stuff should be separate.'

PE and sport:
'Girls shouldn't say ballet dancing is only for girls – boys can do it too.'

'My friend's mum is good at sports. I have a sticker of "My Little Pony" on my Xbox. It doesn't matter what you like, just be yourself.'

'I think boys would feel left out if they were treated like that [not allowed to do ballet]. There shouldn't be such thing as a tomboy and no such thing as girl and boy things.'

'Girls like gymnastics. Boys like boys' things – it shouldn't be like that.'

'I disagree about tomboys. Some people think that boys and girls things are separate. It depends on people's thinking – if they believe there are separate girls and boys things or not.'

'I like football and girls do too. Boys might like ballet or gymnastics.'

Clothes:
'I don't always like girls' clothes. Girls should have the right to pick boys' stuff. It's the same for boys.'

'My cousins dress up. The boys dress up in dresses and make-up. Girls sometimes put boys' clothes on.'

'My brother used to like wearing princess clothes.'

General comments:

'There is no difference between girls and boys – they should like whatever they want. They should be able to play with whatever they want.'

'I think there should be a mix-up in shops with toys and clothes. I think there should be no such thing as a tomboy; it could be a boy or a girl. You should get what you want.'

'I have a t-shirt with pink on it. My mum likes blue. My sister plays football.'

ACTIVITY 4: ACCOUNT OF A LESSON ON GENDER ROLES AND THE THEATRE

Curriculum links: Arts, English

Following a session on *Commedia dell'arte*, as part of the class' One World Week work on Italy, roles that men and women play in the theatre were explored. The children were given two sheets of paper, one with the word 'boy' and one with the word 'girl', and asked to write down anything that they associated with being a girl or a boy.

Some of the written comments were:

BOYS' WRITTEN COMMENTS

- Boys can put make-up on if they're dressing up as a girl.
- Boys like football, rugby, basketball and video games.
- Boys can be cheeky and sneaky.
- Karate, tennis, hockey, acting, watching TV, singing, running, sewing, hair gel, football, cars, rugby, racing.
- In the olden times, only men were allowed to act.
- Some boys like football, rugby and playing tag.

Girl's written comments

- Girls and boys don't have to do separate sports.
- Girls can dress up as boys.
- Violin, badminton, flowers, art, ponies, ballet, singing, music, teddies, knitting, animals, football, gymnastics.
- I like being a girl because we get to wear lots of nice dresses.
- I like football, even though I'm a girl.
- Some girls like boyish things.
- Girls like to dress nice. They also like playing with dolls and princesses.
- Sometimes boys can't understand them.

The children were then given the opportunity to walk around the classroom, looking at images of girls playing football and climbing trees, girls dressed as knights, boys in dresses and kilts, pantomime dames and women in suits.

They were asked five questions and asked to stand on a continuum line to show whether they thought the answer was 'yes', 'no' or 'in between/undecided'. The following are some of their comments.

1. Do you feel happy playing with girls and boys?

   'Yes, I'm happy playing with both boys and girls. Boys are just like girls.'(Girl)

   'I'm not sure, I don't play with girls. I prefer rough games and football.' (Boy)

2. Do you mind if people are tomboys?

   'I don't want to play with tomboys, I don't want to play rough.' (Girl)

   'I play football, I like playing rough games and games with boys. I play tennis with my dad.' (Girl)

3. Do you think it's okay for women to wear suits?

   'I don't know if women should wear suits.' (Girl)

'Yes, I bought a suit on holiday.' (Girl)

'No, it looks really weird.' (Girl)

4. Do you think it's okay for men to wear skirts (kilts)?

'No, my brother wore a skirt and it looked weird. People laughed.' (Girl)

'Yes, boys wear a dress at their christening.' (Boy)

'Yes, I've seen a boy wearing a skirt with shorts. He didn't look silly.' (Girl)

'Maybe. It doesn't look silly. I'm not sure if they should wear it.' (Girl)

5. Do you think it's okay for men to be pantomime dames?

'Yes, it's okay for men to dress up as ladies. If there's no other option, men have to do it.' (Girl)

'No, men have to put make up on and everyone laughs at them.' (Girl)

The children then developed their own questions and chose this question for their philosophical enquiry:

'Is it okay for girls to do boys' things and boys to do girls' things?'

GIRLS' COMMENTS

- 'All girls don't have to do girl things.'
- 'It's okay for girls and boys to play together. Some girls are tomboys, they like playing football and rugby.'
- 'I don't like playing rough stuff, it can hurt people.'
- 'Girls and boys should do both. Some boys like doing gymnastics, some girls like playing football. You can play what you like, but not rough because you could break something.'
- 'At playtime I play a boys' game with my friend (who's a boy).'
- 'When we're outside, everyone can play together. They can pick which game they want to play.'

Boys' COMMENTS

- 'I mind because I'm a boy. I don't want to play princesses or Barbie or other girl things. I like football [disagreement from girls, who said they don't all like to play princesses].'

- 'Boys and girls can do whatever they want. Parcours is like gymnastics. I like that. Girls like riding bikes, some boys like gymnastics.'

- 'Girls and boys can play anything they want. My little brother loves gymnastics. I like video games, gymnastics and dancing. I like being creative, like some girls do.'

- 'Boys can play girls' games and girls can play boys' games. Some girls play football, boys can do gymnastics.'

- 'Some girls like to play boy things and some like to play girl stuff – it's whatever they want. They can choose their own life. They are free to do whatever they want.'

As a follow-up, the children were asked to write down their thoughts about the question in their 'Philosophy jotters'.

Girls' WRITTEN COMMENTS

- If a girl likes football, then she can do it because she might be a tomboy. She doesn't have to be friends with girls, she can be friends with boys because you might play football with boys and make friends with them as well as girls. Girls can also do rugby better because my friend plays rugby and cricket.

- I think it's okay because I like doing boys' things.

- Girls are allowed to play with boys because there is no difference. Only some boys like football and some girls like gymnastics.

- You are free to do whatever you want.

- I think girls are allowed to wear boys' clothes because I'm a girl and I wear boys' clothes.

- I think that girls can play football. Girls can climb trees. Girls can play with boys.

BOYS' WRITTEN COMMENTS

- It's okay because I have played Barbie and my sister has played Jurassic Park when I was little.

- Some girls like playing girl stuff but they might have a best friend who is a boy.

- It's okay for girls to do boys' things because everyone can live their own life.

- I think there are no boys' things or girls' things because I am a boy and I like gymnastics and I have friends who are girls and they like rugby and tennis.

- I think girls and boys have the right to do anything they want. They have a decision and they can do gymnastics if they want to. They have the option to do whatever they like. Girls can play boys' stuff and boys can play girls' stuff.

GENDER AND WORK

ACTIVITY 1: GENDER AND WORK

Summary: A series of lessons for students aged 7–11 exploring the concepts of fairness, equality and gender, along with future career aspirations.

Curriculum links: Mathematics (statistics), English, ICT, PSHE, P4C

LESSON 1: GENDER ROLES IN THE HOME

Purpose: To explore who does what jobs (paid and unpaid) in the students' households.

Resources: 'Who does which jobs in your home?' questionnaire (Table 7.4), graph paper for bar charts.

Procedure:

Prior to this lesson, send home a survey which asks students to find out what jobs their family and friends do and who does the housework (see Table 7.4).

In the lesson, share the results and ask the students to create a bar chart showing who does the most housework.

Table 7.4 Who does which jobs in your home?

Paid work (name jobs and people doing them)				
Unpaid work	**Male**	**Female**	**Both**	**Comments**
Childcare				
Cooking				
Laying the table for meals				
Making beds				
Shopping				
Cleaning bathrooms				
Vacuum cleaning				
Washing clothes				
Ironing				
Emptying bins				
Recycling				
Tidying up				
DIY				
Changing beds				

cont.

Unpaid work	Male	Female	Both	Comments
Cleaning out cupboards				
Cleaning windows				
Sewing repairs				

LESSON 2: WOMEN IN PUBLIC LIFE

Purpose: To analyse data to find out about trends in women's employment over a period of time.

Resources: Graphs and data, questions for each set of data.

Procedure:
Ask the children to read and analyse the information.[6] Set some questions as a guide. For example:

Table 7.5 Women in the police, England and Wales, 2003–2017

As of March every year		Female	
	Total strength	Number	Percentage of total
2003	132,509	25,139	19.0
2004	138,468	27,925	20.2
2005	141,059	29,940	21.2
2006	141,523	31,520	22.3
2007	151,892	33,117	21.8
2008	141,859	34,332	24.2
2009	143,770	36,121	25.1
2010	143,734	36,998	25.7
2011	139,110	36,532	26.3
2012	134,101	35,692	26.8
2013	129,956	35,471	27.3
2014	127,909	35,653	27.9
2015	126,818	35,738	28.2
2016	124,066	35,498	28.6
2017	123,142	35,844	29.1

Source: Police workforce, England and Wales, various years

Women in the police, England and Wales, 2003–2017

1. What percentage of the police force was female in 2003?

2. How many (number) were female in 2010?

3. How many (number) were female in 2017?

4. What percentage was female in 2017?

5. Has the number of women in the police force increased or decreased over time?

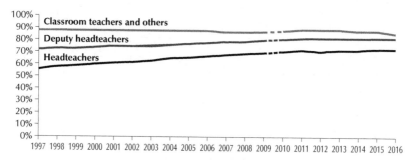

Figure 7.2 Women in primary and nursery education (England), 1997–2016
Source: DfE, school workforce in England, various years.

Women in primary and nursery education (England), 1997–2016

1. Has the percentage of female headteachers in primary and nursery schools increased or decreased or stayed the same over time?

2. Is there a higher percentage of female headteachers or classroom teachers in primary and nursery education?

3. What was the percentage of female headteachers in 1997?

4. What was the percentage of female deputy headteachers in 2009?

5. What was the percentage of female classroom teachers in 2016?

6. Has the percentage of female classroom teachers in primary and nursery education increased or decreased or stayed the same over time?

Table 7.6 Women in the armed forces, 1997–2017

%

	1997	1998	1999	2000	2001	2002	2003	2004	2005	2006	2007	2008	2009	2010	2011	2012	2013	2014	2015	2016	2017
Army																					
Officers	7.7	8.4	8.7	9.2	9.5	9.8	10.2	10.3	10.6	10.8	11.1	11.3	11.2	11.3	11.3	11.6	11.9	11.8	11.9	11.8	11.8
Other ranks	5.9	6.5	6.7	6.8	6.7	6.8	7.0	7.0	7.0	7.1	7.2	7.3	7.3	7.3	7.4	7.7	8.0	8.2	8.4	8.5	8.6
All	6.1	6.8	7.0	7.1	7.1	7.2	7.4	7.5	7.5	7.6	7.7	7.8	7.8	7.9	8.0	8.2	8.5	8.7	9.0	9.0	9.1
Naval Service																					
Officers	5.6	5.8	6.1	6.8	7.2	7.6	7.8	8.2	8.5	8.9	9.0	9.4	9.7	9.7	9.7	9.7	9.9	10.0	10.2	10.4	10.8
Other ranks	7.5	7.7	8.0	8.2	8.4	8.7	9.1	9.3	9.4	9.5	9.5	9.6	9.5	9.6	9.3	9.1	8.8	8.8	9.1	9.1	8.9
All	7.2	7.3	7.6	8.0	8.2	8.5	8.9	9.1	9.2	9.3	9.4	9.5	9.6	9.6	9.4	9.2	9.0	9.1	9.3	9.3	9.3
RAF																					
Officers	8.0	8.6	9.2	10.0	10.6	11.1	11.6	12.4	13.1	13.7	14.3	14.7	15.3	15.4	15.7	15.9	16.4	16.5	16.5	16.7	16.9
Other ranks	8.8	9.1	9.4	9.7	10.1	10.5	11.0	11.5	11.8	12.0	12.4	12.7	13.0	13.2	13.2	13.2	13.2	13.0	13.2	13.2	13.2
All	8.6	9.0	9.3	9.8	10.2	10.6	11.1	11.7	12.1	12.3	12.8	13.2	13.5	13.7	13.8	13.9	13.9	13.8	13.9	14.0	14.0
Overall																					
Officers	7.3	7.8	8.3	8.9	9.3	9.7	10.1	10.5	10.9	11.3	11.6	11.9	12.1	12.2	12.0	12.4	12.6	12.7	12.7	12.8	13.0
Other ranks	7.0	7.4	7.6	7.8	7.9	8.1	8.4	8.6	8.7	8.7	8.8	8.9	9.0	9.0	9.1	9.1	9.2	9.3	9.6	9.6	9.6
All	7.0	7.5	7.7	8.0	8.1	8.3	8.7	8.9	9.0	9.1	9.3	9.4	9.5	9.6	9.7	9.7	9.8	9.9.	10.1	10.2	10.2

Source: Defense personnel statistics, various years, as of April each year

Women in the armed forces, 1997–2017

1. What percentage were female army officers in 2017?

2. What percentage of the navy was female in 2000?

3. What percentage of the RAF was female in 1997?

4. What percentage of the RAF was female in 2017?

5. Has the overall percentage of women in the armed forces increased or decreased?

6. Create three of your own questions about the table.

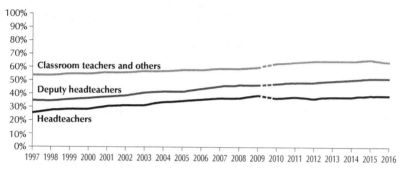

Figure 7.3 Women in secondary education (England), 1997–2016
Source: DfE, school workforce in England, various years.

Women in secondary education (England), 1997–2016

1. Has the percentage of female headteachers in secondary education increased or decreased or stayed the same over time?

2. Is there a higher percentage of female headteachers or classroom teachers in secondary education?

3. What was the percentage of female headteachers in 1997?

4. What was the percentage of female deputy headteachers in 2009?

5. What was the percentage of female classroom teachers in 2006?

6. Has the percentage of female classroom teachers in secondary education increased or decreased or stayed the same over time?

7. Look back at the primary graph. Is there a higher percentage of female headteachers in primary/nursery or secondary education?

8. Is there a higher percentage of female class teachers in primary/nursery or secondary education?

9. Create five of your own questions about both graphs.

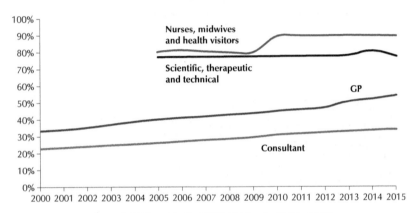

Figure 7.4 Women in the NHS (England), 2000–2015
Source: NHS Information Centre, NHS workforce statistics in England, various years.

Women in the NHS (England), 2000–2015

1. What percentage of women was consultants in 2000? Has this percentage increased or decreased?

2. What percentage of GPs was female in 2015? Has this percentage increased or decreased since 2000?

3. What happened to the percentage of female nurses, midwives, and health visitors in 2009?

4. What happened to the percentage of female nurses, midwives and health visitors in 2010?

5. What percentage of nurses, midwives and health visitors was female in 2015?

6. Why do you think the top two data lines don't start until 2005?

7. Create three questions about this data.

You will notice that generally the percentage of women is increasing in some professions (primary and secondary education, NHS, police and armed forces).

Follow up with a discussion about what the graphs show overall. Ask the students if there are any surprises and why they think certain jobs have more men or women.

LESSON 3: FUTURE CAREERS QUESTIONNAIRE

Purpose: For children to consider what job they might like to do in the future.

Resources: Questions in a PowerPoint presentation.

Procedure:
After the discussion generated in Lesson 2, ask the students to think about the following questions:

1. If you could choose up to three jobs to do when you're older, what would they be?

2. What do you think you need to do to get that job?

3. Is there anything that might stop you from doing your dream job?

4. Do you think there are more men or women doing your dream job at the moment?

5. Would you be happiest working with people of the same gender, a different gender or a mix?

LESSON 4: P4C ABOUT GENDER AND WORK STEREOTYPES

Purpose: To challenge the students' perceptions about which jobs women and men can do.

Resources: Photographs of people in non-stereotypical careers for their gender.

Procedure:
Use photographs that question gender roles in jobs as a stimulus (for example, men doing housework, women in the army, male nurses). In small groups, the students sort the images and discuss their criteria for sorting them. Examples of the categories that the students might sort the images into are: images showing jobs that involve caring for others/jobs that involve working with other people but not in a caring role/jobs where people work on their own; images showing jobs in STEM/jobs not in STEM; images which are surprising/expected, etc. Ask questions such as:

1. What are your categories?

2. Why did you choose them?

3. How are they different from other groups?

4. Are there any photographs that could go in two or more categories?

5. Does anyone want to challenge another group's classification and move one of their photographs?

Initiate a P4C discussion by asking the students to generate a philosophical question and choose one as a class. The students should then sit in a circle to share their thoughts and ideas on the chosen question.

LESSON 5: VISITOR

Purpose: To think about non-stereotyped careers and to find out more about careers.

Resources: Visitor, dressing-up clothes, BBC Newsround clip, 'Builder inspires kids to look at all jobs in the future'[7] or Equality and Human Rights Commission's 'Pass it on'.[8]

Procedure:
For this lesson you may wish to invite an external speaker who has expertise in, or personal experience of, entering male or female-dominated careers.

Begin by showing the BBC Newsround clip 'Builder inspires kids to look at all jobs in the future' or 'Pass it on', a film by the Equality and Human Rights Commission which aims to 'inspire children and encourage them to think about their future, as well as challenging stereotypical thinking around certain jobs'.

Follow this up by getting some of the students to dress up as firefighters, police officers, Red Cross volunteers, builders, bus drivers or doctors, and ask them to stand on a continuum line according to whether they think the job is just for boys, girls or somewhere in the middle. Ask the students to generate questions for the visitor to find out more about their job.

LESSON 6: P4C ABOUT GENDER AND WORK STEREOTYPES

Purpose: To think more deeply about gender stereotyping and careers.

Resources: Paper and pens.

Procedure:
Remind students of all the lessons completed so far. In order to reflect on what they have learnt, ask them to use their thoughts as stimuli and to come up with a philosophical question they would like to discuss further.

Examples may include:

- Do you think that boys and girls should have the same responsibilities within the same job?

- Why do you think that there are jobs for boys and jobs for girls?

LESSON 7: LEARNING MORE ABOUT CAREERS

Purpose: To find out about possible jobs suited to experiences and skills.

Resources: PCs, laptops or tablets – one each or one between two, 'Gender and work job research' writing frame (Table 7.7), 'Gender and work job application form' writing frame (Table 7.8).

Table 7.7 Gender and work job research

Job research
Job title:
Their work may involve:
How they work:
Where they work:
Other related jobs in the field:
Qualifications and experience needed:

Table 7.8 Gender and work job application form

Job application form
Name:
Job title:
1. Introduction (briefly outline your skills and why you want the job):
2. Why would you like to have this job? (Write more detail here, e.g. interested in this area, want to work with people, exciting opportunities):
3. What have you done in the past that will help you do this job well? (Hobbies, after-school clubs, extra projects):
4. What strengths/skills do you have to help you do this job well? (Good at maths, sport, team work, listening, leading others, confident):
5. What do you think the job involves? (Key responsibilities, where you would work, how you would work):
Signature:

Procedure:

Using a PC, laptop or tablet, ask the students to do an interactive quiz[9] on which job they could be suitable for in the future.

Ask the students to research what they would need to do to get that job and what the job is like.[10] They could use the 'Gender and work job research' writing frame (Table 7.7).

Students write an application form for their chosen job using the 'Gender and work job application form' writing frame (Table 7.8) and practise interview techniques. Use the National Careers website[11] for information on writing CVs and interview questions and techniques.

The teacher or the students choose a number of candidates to take through to interview for their chosen jobs. Unsuccessful candidates form an interview panel for each job and create a set of interview questions whilst the candidates prepare for their interview.

ADDITIONAL ACTIVITY

Organise a school jobs fair where men and women are invited to represent roles not traditional for their gender.

> One of the Gender Respect Project teachers who organised a jobs fair said, 'The children were enthused and engaged and their understanding, particularly about police officers, was success-fully challenged. Many children expressed the fact that their understanding had been altered and almost all children said that they would like to have one of the roles that they learned about.'

EVALUATION

Ask students to redo Lesson 3 to see whether their ideas have changed.

Use the 'Gender and work evaluation form' (Table 7.9) to reflect further on the activities.

Table 7.9 Gender and work evaluation

1. How much did you enjoy the following activities? Rate them from 1 to 5 (1 = not at all, 5 = enjoyed it a lot)					
Questions about graphs that showed how many men and women do certain jobs	1	2	3	4	5
P4C using photographs of men and women doing non-stereotypical jobs	1	2	3	4	5
A visitor	1	2	3	4	5
Research about your future career options	1	2	3	4	5
2. What have you learned from our work about jobs and gender stereotypes?					
3. If you were a teacher, what would you do to teach children about jobs and gender stereotypes?					

GENDER AND SPORT

Summary and purpose: A lesson using P4C to challenge students' stereotypes in relation to sport and gender.

Curriculum links: PSHE, English, P4C

Resources: Clips from the films *Billy Elliot* (Daldry 2000) and *Bend it like Beckham* (Chadha 2002); images of women and men doing a variety of sports; newspaper articles: female boxing was allowed in the Olympics in 2012 for the first time; differences between men and women's gymnastics; women in Saudi Arabia are not allowed to play sport, etc.

Procedure:

1. Warm up: Create an imaginary line in the classroom with one end as 'male' and the other as 'female'. Name a sport and students have to go with the first thing they think as to where they would stand on the line: do they think of the sport as a male sport, a female sport, equally for both or somewhere in between?

Stimuli: See 'Resources' above.

2. Generate questions: Encourage students to write their thoughts down as they consider the different stimuli. They should generate a philosophical question that they would like to discuss relating to the stimuli.

As a group they choose one question. The groups' questions are written on the board and explained by each group. All students close their eyes and the teacher reads out the questions. Students put up their hands for the one they would like to discuss.

Students are reminded of the rules of P4C (for example, take turns speaking, listen carefully, respect, etc.).

3. First thoughts: Ask students to write down their initial thoughts.

4. Building: Choose someone to start the discussion then encourage students to listen carefully and critically and to respond to one another with sentence openers such as: 'I agree/disagree with…' 'I think that…' 'Building on what…has said…I have a new point'.

5. Last words: Go round the circle giving everyone the opportunity to give their final thoughts using the sentence opener 'I wonder if…'

**EXAMPLES OF QUESTIONS GENERATED
IN A YEAR 3 ENQUIRY**

- Why can't all genders do some sports?

- Why do people think boys can't do girls' things and girls can't do boys' things?

- Why do people not like boys to do ballet?

- Why can't women play every sport? (Question chosen)

- Why do men and women have different equipment for gymnastics?

Girls' comments:

'Girls like shopping, boys like running. That is why some people think that girls can't play sports.'

'Some people let girls play, others think boys are stronger and faster so only they can play.'

'Some girls can be stronger than boys... I think that all boys should think that if they were a girl if they would like it if they were told they couldn't do this sport. I think everyone should get to choose if they can do it or not.'

Boys' comments:

'Men have skill and speed in football.'

'Men are stronger than women...men and ladies are good at dancing.'

'Why don't boys do girls' sports?'

'Girls can play football because they are strong.'

'Women are more into swimming than men. Because women don't just want to get strong. They want to get fit and healthy as well, like boys.'

**EXAMPLES OF QUESTIONS GENERATED
IN A YEAR 5 ENQUIRY**

- Why aren't women seen on TV as much as men?

- Why do you barely ever hear about women sports people?

- Why do people think that men are better and stronger at sport than women?

- Why can't there be some sports for men, some for women and some for both? (Question chosen)

- Why should different genders affect how we play sport?

Boys' comments:

'You have to practice to get better at sport, regardless of gender.'

'If women's rugby was on TV more, more women would want to join in.'

'I disagree. I think some sports, for example, synchronised swimming are for girls and some, for example, football, are for boys.'

Girls' comments:

'Some people think girls are better than boys, or boys are better than girls in general life. It's the same for sport.'

IDENTITY, BODY IMAGE AND RELATIONSHIPS

Summary and purpose: This is a series of three lessons on body image and relationships for students aged 9–11.

Curriculum links: PSHE, RSE, Art, English

LESSON 1: WHO AM I?

Purpose: To start thinking about personal identity.

Resources: Films about identity as stimuli for ideas:

'Def poetry' – www.youtube.com/watch?v=VuAbGJBvIVY

'To this day' – www.youtube.com/watch?v=Itun92DfnPY (start at five minutes to skip swear word use. N.B. mentions suicide and medication)[12]

'I am not my hair' – www.youtube.com/watch?v=0t9E_7Qk7os

Mirrors, pictures of abstract portraits (by, for example, Picasso), art materials.

Procedure:
Introduce the topic by sharing the three YouTube clips above.

- Discuss in pairs and then as a class: What do these songs/poems have in common? What were some key messages you noticed? What are these songs/poems saying about body image?

- Give out mirrors. Ask students to think quietly to themselves about what they can see. What kind of a person do they recognise? What is the person good at? What are they known for? Encourage them to think about who they really are and what they may want to be in the future. Perhaps invite students to share their thoughts, if they wish, with the person next to them.

- Show a range of abstract portraits, some done by children. What is unusual about these portraits? Ask students to feed back their ideas to the whole group. Ask them to draw a self-portrait of what they think they may look like, in the style of Picasso, adding their likes and dislikes. This portrait will not just resemble them – it will represent them.

LESSON 2: HEALTHY AND UNHEALTHY RELATIONSHIPS

Purpose: To recognise what constitutes a healthy relationship and how some relationships can be unhealthy.

Resources: Images showing different kinds of relationships and families, sticky notes, wedding photos from a domestic violence campaign.[13]

Procedure:

1. Explain that we will be discussing relationships. Ask what different kinds of relationships exist. Show images of a range of 'standard' and 'non-standard' relationships and families – which is 'normal'? Discuss and feed back.

2. What do we think makes a relationship 'normal' and stable? Work in pairs to sort scenarios into healthy/unhealthy relationships. Feed back. For 'unhealthy' grouping, does this mean that all of these things will happen in the families which we think are NOT normal? Discuss: does this change our thinking? If so, how?

3. On sticky notes in groups, write the qualities of healthy relationships. Rank them into a diamond nine and share the group's reasoning with the rest of the class. Discuss: How much should you change in a relationship? Should you change at all?

4. Thinking about all of the discussions and the qualities of a relationship that they have come up with, students spend 20 minutes writing a description of a perfect relationship in their books. Tell them that if discussing male/female relationships makes them feel uncomfortable, they can refer to different relationships in their writing.

5. Plenary discussion: Search on the internet for 'wedding photo from domestic violence campaign'.[14] Show students the front and back view. Is this 'normal' or healthy? What does it teach us? What would you say to someone who thinks they know what a 'normal' relationship looks like?

LESSON 3: BODY IMAGE

Purpose: To recognise that pressure to behave in a risky or unhealthy way can come from a variety of sources or people.

Resources: Magazine front covers, A3 paper, examples of Photoshopped photographs, Dove 'Evolution' clip.[15]

Procedure:

1. Look at a range of magazine front covers. Discuss in pairs – what messages do students think they give us? Work in separate sex groups for comfort and confidence.

2. On large A3 outlines of bodies, each group labels the parts of the body that they think are important to be 'perfect' (for example, straight teeth, small ears). Feed back to the class for the other gender to hear.

3. Show students some Photoshopped photos. Identify which is the real person. Why do you think the magazine has changed them? Do you think there is anything wrong with the 'before'?

4. Play the Dove 'Evolution' clip. What do students think now? Discuss these questions: What can affect body image and what people think is beautiful? Why does the media portray 'beautiful' people?

5. Students complete these sentences in their 'Philosophy jotters':

   • I think that the media does/does not affect people's ideas about body image because...

   • One thing I have realised that I didn't know at the start of this lesson is...

   • One thing I would change about the way the media deals with things like body image is...

VIOLENCE AND PREJUDICE[16] (SUE LYLE)

Summary and purpose: A series of five lessons on the theme of violence and prejudice for students aged ten and upwards intended to promote a discussion of values and promote principles of respect between young people and active participation.

Curriculum links: PSHE, RSE, English

Finding relevant and interesting talking points: Select a topic from the following list that a pilot group of teachers identified as affecting girls and young women in particular: 'girlification', sexualisation of girls, the pressure to achieve highly, class differences, search for the perfect body, dieting, violence against girls and women. Depending on their social, cultural, economic and historical circumstances, young people experience different 'realities'. They live in different environments, have access to different amounts of wealth, live in different kinds of families, some come from minority ethnic groups and some have disabilities – all of these factors will impact on how they respond to the images. Young people will have different sexualities and different religious beliefs that will also impact on their thinking. This diversity is why Sue Lyle decided to leave it up to teachers to choose the images they think will best facilitate the activities for the young people they work with.

An internet image search is generally a good place to start. Key search terms might include:

- 'Girls and pink toys' – for use when discussing 'girlification' (even just searching 'girls' toys' brings up a mass of pink and sparkly items).

- 'Sexualisation' or 'sexualisation of children' – will bring up images where young children have been dressed to look like teenagers or posed provocatively.

- 'Sexist adverts' – will bring up images of objectified women, among which you'll find many legitimate adverts and promotional materials.

- 'Violence against girls' or 'violence against women' – shows campaign posters and photos taken to highlight the issue ('violence against men' might also bring up some interesting images).

- 'Women should' – typing this into an internet image search brings up an interesting photo campaign depicting popular searches beginning with 'Women should...' 'Women shouldn't...' 'Women cannot...', etc.; most are derogatory.

- 'High achieving girls' or 'high achieving women' – the former shows girls receiving good grades, girls in graduating robes and caps, girls taking part in projects and so on, while the latter generally brings up images of professional women.

- 'Gender' – lots of cartoons here, most commenting on sexist stereotypes and transgender issues.

- 'Anorexia', 'dieting', 'body dysmorphia', 'perfect body shape', 'insecurity', etc. – all bring up many images to choose from relating to these topics.

- 'Sexism against men/women', 'misogyny', 'male/female stereo-types' – will display interesting images, cartoons and memes to do with sexism towards men and women.

- 'Young people/teens/children' in conjunction with 'poor', 'disadvantaged', 'homeless', 'no jobs', 'streets', etc. – brings up images of teenagers out on the streets, drinking, vandalism, teen mothers, young people queuing at job centres, poor living conditions, etc.

You will need a minimum of 15 images for a class of 30 students.

LESSON 1: MAKING CONNECTIONS

Purpose: To introduce the images to the group. To encourage them to listen to each other's ideas and make connections between them.

Resources: A set of images downloaded and printed from the internet, each one mounted in the centre of a sheet of A3 paper to allow mark making on the sheet around it in response to the images.

Procedure:

1. Put mounted images on display. Ask the students to look at them and pick one that they find interesting or puzzling. They can indicate their interest by making a mark on the mounting sheet.

2. Ask the students to stand together around the image they have chosen and share their reasons for choosing it.

3. Afterwards, ask them to give an overview of their discussions to the rest of the class. What similarities and differences did they identify in their thinking?

LESSON 2: ASKING QUESTIONS

Purpose: To get the students used to asking questions about the images. To help them see that some question stems are more fruitful than others in generating discussion of ideas and concepts.

Resources: Enough images to have one per group of three in the class. A set of question words, for example, what, where, when, why, how, who, could, should, would, is, can, does, if.

Procedure:

1. Give out one image at random to each group of three. Give each group three of the question words. Ask each group to come up with at least one question about their image for each of the question words they have been given.

2. Ask each group to show their picture to the group and read out one of their questions. Ask the class to identify what type of question it is. Closed? Open? Thinking?

   - A closed question will have one right answer that may be answered from the picture or might need some research.

   - An open question is speculative or hypothetical – it requires imagination to try and answer it. Such questions reveal the students' assumptions about the images.

   - Thinking questions invite the exploration of concepts, in particular with the use of 'should', which indicate a moral concept. These are particularly important when looking at issues depicted in the images.

3. Ask them which question words have produced the most interesting questions and discuss why.

4. Back in their groups, ask them to formulate a 'should' question for their picture. Ask them to read them aloud. Point out that most 'should' questions have a moral element – emphasise that the issues raised by the images have ethical implications.

LESSON 3: MOST/LEAST LIKE A CHILD

Purpose: To explore students' ideas of what it means to be a child using images.

Resources: Set of images depicting children and young people.

Procedure:
STAGE 1:

1. Students work in pairs to consider the following questions as a warm-up for the main activity:

   - How old are you?

   - How old will you be when you are an adult?

   - What does it mean to be an adult?

2. Ask students to feed back their answers to the last two, to see the variety of opinions.

STAGE 2

3. Make sure there are enough images to allow students to work in pairs. Randomly allocate a picture to each pair.

4. Set up a concept line using a skipping rope – one end represents 'Most like a child', the other end, 'Least like a child'.

5. Ask each pair to decide where to place their picture on the rope. The students then work as a whole class to negotiate a rank order for all the pictures according to where they are between 'Most like a child' and 'Least like a child'. Ask them to justify the position in which they place their picture and be prepared to change their minds as they listen to the reasons given by their peers. Emphasise that there are no right or wrong answers, but they must be able to support their views with reasons.

LESSON 4: MATCHING

Purpose: To consider some current research on the position of young people today.

Resources: Set of cards with research information printed on them (see 'Research Information for Cards'). Use one bullet point for each card.

Procedure:

1. Students work in groups of two or three. Give each group a set of research information and ask them to decide on which pictures to place the information. Do they all put the same cards on the same pictures? (There are no right answers.) They should justify where they have put the pictures.

2. Having placed the research information with the pictures, ask the students to work in groups of four or five and pick one picture and the research information to look at. Ask them to consider what they think the implications of the research information are for young people today.

    You may not wish to use all the research cards – select to suit your purpose.

RESEARCH INFORMATION FOR CARDS

- Girls as young as five are worrying about their weight (APPG 2012).

- Half of girls and up to one-third of boys have dieted to lose weight (APPG 2012).

- 17% of girls aged 7–10 felt they should lose weight and this rose to 54% for those aged 11–16 and 66% of those aged 17–21 (Girlguiding 2016).

- In 2011, 73% of girls aged 7–21 were happy with how they looked, falling to 61% in 2017 (Girlguiding 2016).

- 71% of all 16- to 18-year-olds (boys and girls) say they hear sexual name-calling with terms such as 'slut' or 'slag' towards girls at schools daily or a few times a week (End Violence Against Women 2017).

- 22% of girls aged 7–12 had experienced jokes of a sexual nature from boys; 12% of girls had seen rude pictures or rude graffiti about girls and women; 10% had experienced unwanted touching (Girlguiding 2016).

- Women working full time in the UK in 2017 earned 13.9% less than men (The Fawcett Society 2017b).

- 63% of men think their arms or chests are not muscular enough (UWE 2012).

LESSON 5: GENERATING QUESTIONS

Purpose: For students to generate their own questions about a specific image (from the selection of questions used in Lesson 3).

Resources: Display all the images – make sure they are numbered.

Procedure:

STAGE 1: CHOOSING PICTURES

Ask the students to view the images individually and take a note of the number of one they would like to ask more questions about.

Find out if anyone has chosen the same one as someone else and put those who have chosen the same pictures together in pairs. Pair up the rest of the students. Ask each pair to discuss their choice or choices of picture and say why they want to generate more questions about the picture. Ask them to choose just one picture between them (if their pictures are not identical). (They could decide to use a different picture if they wish.)

STAGE 2: GENERATING QUESTIONS

Join pairs together to form groups of four. Ask them to discuss their two chosen pictures and again decide on one picture they would like to spend time discussing.

Allow each group to collect their picture (be prepared for some groups choosing the same picture; you may need a second copy). They should write a title for the picture in the middle of their sheet.

Ask them to brainstorm as many questions as they can around the picture.

STAGE 3: CLASSIFICATION OF QUESTIONS

Pass the pictures and sets of questions on to the next group in a clockwise direction. Ask the new group to look at the picture and questions generated and classify the questions. Are they:

- Closed questions – with one right answer that can be researched?

- Open questions – which could have a range of answers?

- Thinking questions – questions which are about concepts (for example, justice – is it fair for...to...?) or a moral issue (Should...)?

Ask them to put a tick by closed questions, a smiley face by open questions and a smiley face with a question mark above it next to thinking questions.

Discuss the questions. Ask the groups to report on the thinking questions (assuming they have some). What makes these thinking questions?

STAGE 4: CONCENTRIC CIRCLES

To test out the quality of the 'thinking questions', ask students to form two circles – an inner and an outer circle. Ask those in the inner circle to turn round to face someone in the outer circle (if numbers aren't even, you may need one group of three).

Taking each of the young people's 'thinking questions' in turn, and making sure the children can see the picture to which each question relates (these can be displayed on a whiteboard), read them aloud and give them one to two minutes to try to answer the question in their pairs. Call 'stop!' and ask students in the inner circle to move one person to the left. They will each now have a new partner. Read out the next 'thinking question' and give them another one to two minutes to discuss it in pairs. Repeat until at least one 'thinking question' from each group has been discussed.

STAGE 5: CHOOSING AND DISCUSSING A QUESTION

Write each of the questions the students have discussed on a sheet of A4-sized paper and place them so everyone can see them.

Read all the questions in turn once. Then explain to the students that they are going to vote for one question they would like to discuss as a whole group. This should be a secret ballot. Ask them all to close their eyes at the same time. Read each question aloud and ask for votes by a show of hands.

When a question has been chosen, discuss it using P4C with the class.

TAKING ACTION

- Pupil conferences

- One Billion Rising action

- Other suggestions for how students can take action

- Other resources for discussing gender issues with children

It may be that the experience of exploring gender issues, using the methods outlined, will motivate students to want to find a way of making a change. It was recognised in the Gender Respect Project that unless children are given an opportunity to do something about the issues that they care about, then this can lead to a feeling of powerlessness. Some accounts with lesson plans and resources of how children were supported to make changes in their schools during the project are mentioned below. It is important for genuine pupil participation that action arises from the children's own concerns and passions and that they are supported by adults to carry these out. Roger Hart's 'Ladder of Participation' illustrates this idea. The lower three rungs of the ladder are not considered as participation by Hart. It is only at rung 4 where participation can really begin. In the Gender Respect Project we were aiming for participation at a level between 7 and 8 where children and young people are supported by adults to make decisions and take action.

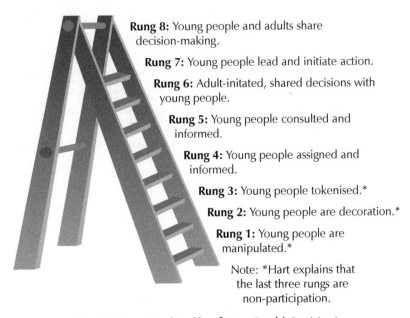

Rung 8: Young people and adults share decision-making.

Rung 7: Young people lead and initiate action.

Rung 6: Adult-initated, shared decisions with young people.

Rung 5: Young people consulted and informed.

Rung 4: Young people assigned and informed.

Rung 3: Young people tokenised.*

Rung 2: Young people are decoration.*

Rung 1: Young people are manipulated.*

Note: *Hart explains that the last three rungs are non-participation.

Figure 7.5 Roger Hart's Ladder of Young People's Participation
Adapted from R. Hart (1992)

PUPIL CONFERENCES

During the final year of the Gender Respect Project we brought together enthusiastic students from each of the project schools (primary and secondary) for two days of workshops separated by a couple of months. At the first conference, in the primary workshop, the students were shown a series of images and phrases showing stereotypical and non-stereotypical images of jobs, emotions and sports. They were asked to choose one in which they felt interested. Some great discussions were had about women in the army, boys dancing, men and women playing football and boys crying. The phrase 'You throw like a girl!' proved to be an interesting one too, with one boy pointing out that this was a compliment as girls throw very well. Students then stood on a continuum line with 'agree' and 'disagree' at either end for the following statements:

Boys are embarrassed to do dance.

Boys are all good at DIY.[17]

There was an interesting gender split with the dance, with the boys saying that they would not be embarrassed to do dance. The general feeling about DIY was that some boys are good at DIY but some certainly are not.

Next the group thought about what was good about being a boy/girl/either. Here are some of their thoughts:

Girls: dance, being smart, people don't judge you when you cry, you can wear trousers and skirts.

Boys: straightforward, self-confident, being smart, dance, nerd, exercise, mathematics.

Either: long and short hair, ability to do sport, sensible, make-up.

The group then discussed the pressures and difficulties of being a boy/girl and wrote them on sticky notes around an outline of a body. These included:

'Boys get teased for dancing.'

'It's harder for girls to do football because they're not as good as boys.'

'Girls should get the right amount of money for doing the same job.'

'Some boys think that they're superior to everyone else.'

'Boys find it hard to cry in front of other people.'

'In other countries, boys go to school and girls have to stay at home and work.'

They then ranked these pressures from most to least important, using a diamond nine shape.

Using these ideas, the students worked with their schools to create an action plan of something that they felt needed addressing in school. Two groups wished to create a play to act out in assembly, looking at respect for one another and challenging teasing. The third group wished to organise a dance competition to encourage more boys to have a go at dancing.

Stephen, a teacher from the Gender Respect Project, recounts: 'The four school council members who attended the pupil conference (from our primary school) were buzzing on the train home to Barnsley. I wasn't sure if this was just a feel-good factor or a sustained desire to bring about a change. By Thursday of the following week, they were knocking on the nursery door [Stephen is a nursery teacher] with a list that they had already completed. They explained they had started a presentation, made a poster for around school, were working on leaflets and now needed our headteacher to allocate a whole school assembly.

Our headteacher was delighted and taken aback by their passion. He quickly provided a date for an assembly for them to work towards. Dearne FM, the local radio station, was at school the next day spreading the news about how eager the children were to address Gender Respect.

On the day of the assembly they were very professional, confident and worked clearly in a team to share the message to the rest of school. I'm delighted that the "pupil voice" is now discussing more than dressing-up days and fundraising and that children are supporting their own community by voicing their feelings and desires. It was interesting that, after numerous days working together, the boys didn't show for one of the lunchtime sessions. The girls said that the boys had needed a day to play out and that they had let them. The boys in effect had left the girls to write and design so they could play out. However, the boys still wanted a say when it came to decision-making.

It generated a discussion and I reminded them that we are all in it together with a shared responsibility. You cannot opt out and yet still want a say. They understood the message and recognised that sacrificing playing out is part of teamwork. They agreed that after the assembly they would meet one lunch time a week. They still have the passion for Gender Respect and I'm looking forward to seeing the impact across the school.'

At the second conference the students reported back to each other as a whole group on the actions they had taken. This included a slide show of the boys' dance competition in one school.[18] The primary school students then worked with each other to problem solve around gender-based scenarios which the teachers thought they might encounter at school:

- You are working in a group with two girls and two boys. The boys keep taking the lead, making the decisions and dominating the conversation. What do you do?

- You are a girl and you enjoy playing games and creating a PowerPoint presentation on the computer. One lunchtime, you are working on something and a boy comes over and takes over from you, saying he is just showing you how to do it. What do you do?

- You are a boy and your friend has just hit you on the arm and told you you're no good at running. You begin to cry. Another friend comes over. What happens next?

The students were asked to create a drama showing the scenario and what they would do next. A really interesting discussion about their experiences of these situations and what they did led to some questions to explore in a philosophical enquiry:

- Why is blue seen as a boys' colour and pink seen as a girls' colour?

- Are boys and girls allowed to express their feelings equally?

- Why is it sometimes difficult for boys and girls to be friends?

- Do boys talk louder to make themselves heard?

- Why do people sometimes get teased for doing things that the other gender does?

The question they chose was: 'Why is it sometimes difficult for boys and girls to be friends?' The students said that sometimes they were teased for playing with someone of the opposite gender and people would say that they had a crush on them. They felt that it was unfair and that everyone should be able to play with whomever they wanted to, regardless of gender. They thought they would be more aware of it in school and would challenge people if they heard teasing.

Based on the experiences of a group of students in one of the schools, in the second part of the workshop the group thought about the role of the students as Gender Respect ambassadors. The children came up with a job description together:

- To challenge gender inequality.

- To mediate arguments relating to gender.

- To run workshops to help people understand about gender respect.

- To create materials to raise awareness – posters, songs, PowerPoint presentations.

They also created a vision for the ambassadors:

- We will challenge others if we feel they are being disrespectful.

- All genders will play happily with one another.

- We will have equal participation.

- We will listen respectfully to each other.

- We will ensure our environment and materials reflect gender respect.

Year 3 class's ideas for taking action around gender and sport

Following the activities on gender and sport the students generated suggestions of how girls and boys could be encouraged to play whatever sport they wanted to. They came up with the following ideas:

- Teaching sports to younger children, discussing gender issues.

- Lunchtime sports club.

- After-school club.

- Write a song/poem to persuade children to encourage people to do all sports – for an assembly.

- Posters with messages to go around school.

- Read posters in assembly.

- Rules and facts to go around school, with pictures of different sports.

- Acrostic poem with a message.

- Make a website.

The suggestion of making posters with messages was implemented with a small group of children from across KS2 with a brief from the Year 3 class that came up with the idea.

Success criteria for posters developed by Year 3

- Title

- Pictures – computer, hand

- Slogans

- Messages to encourage people to be kind to others

- Messages to encourage people to 'give it a go' = try other sports

- Information/facts about the sport

- Information about/images of sports legends

- Easy to understand: makes sense

- Flaps, pop-ups

- Our values: cooperation, responsibility, teamwork, and thoughtfulness, respect.

Examples of messages

- Don't tease people.

- Don't be mean if a boy wants to do gymnastics.

- Don't tease people who do different sports to you.

- You have the right to do any sport you choose.

- Don't judge other people by their sport.

- Anyone can do any sports they want to.

- Be fair to girls and boys in sport.

- Let girls and boys join in.

A visiting artist supported the teacher and group of students providing inspiration from a range of paintings by Paul Klee, Henri Matisse, Andy Warhol and Bridget Riley. The group discussed how to create different effects, what gender the person might be or whether they would be non-gender specific and what messages to include.

These are the posters the students developed:

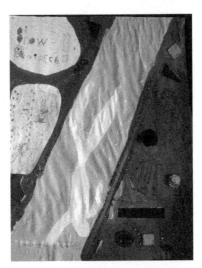

Year 3. Message: Show respect!

Year 4. Message: You have the right to choose your sport

Year 5. Message: Don't feel afraid of doing a sport usually played by the opposite gender, even if people laugh at you

Year 6. Message: Words such as peace, courage, freedom, trust and strength

The students showed their posters in a whole school assembly, just before sports day. They explained why they had created their posters and what the messages were that they had chosen. These posters were displayed in the hall for all students to see.

While they were creating these posters, the class teacher spoke with the students about how they felt about boys and girls doing different sports and whether they thought the posters were effective. These are some of their comments:

Regarding attitudes

- 'Every sport is free for anyone to do.'

- 'You can't just laugh at people for doing different sports.'

- 'No sport is for a boy or a girl, it's an equal choice.'

- 'In secondary schools there is more teasing. They think they are older and smarter.'

- 'It's not fair. We know lots of male footballer names but no one knows the names of women football players.'

- 'It's like racism but with gender.'

- 'People expect boys to play football.'

- 'Boys are rougher than girls. To be rough makes you look really strong. Boys don't realise that some girls like to be rough too.'

- 'Football has always been a more popular sport and people prefer to play football because they get paid lots of money for it.'

- 'Lots of people can play football as you only need a ball and some grass.'

- 'There's one girl in the rugby club. People treat her the same. She fits in.'

Regarding the effectiveness of the posters?

- 'Sometimes if a boy wants to do a "girls" sport, he would feel worried. So something needs to change. The posters are a good idea to help reduce teasing.'

- 'It's a good idea to do the posters, as some people don't think that a boy would do ballet. If you asked "Can boys do ballet?" they would say yes, but they wouldn't think of boys doing ballet.'

- 'The posters will help people to think more about the sports that we can do and help us realise that both genders can do any sports.'

Since the Year 3 class had been involved in the project from the beginning, the class teacher wanted to get their impressions of the posters and see whether they were pleased with them and thought that they were effective. Here are some of their comments:

Regarding attitudes

- 'Let every girl or boy do what they want.'

- 'Don't tease other people about what sport they do.'

Regarding the effectiveness of the posters?

- 'I think the dance one was good because it showed how a boy can dance.'

- 'Good effective messages.'

- 'I like the glitter. It really makes the message stand out.'

- 'The Y6s has lots of values. That's what makes theirs good.'

- 'They show that boys and girls can do whichever sport they want.'

- 'It's a clear message in a stylish way.'

- 'I think the posters were great because they have a very clear message.'

- 'I like the idea of a poster with a message on it.'

- 'I like the part of the poster that says even if you get teased, stay strong.'

- 'I think the posters are very good because every poster has an important and clear message.'

- 'They were very good because it should not be girls doing gymnastics. It should be girls and boys doing sports!'

- 'It's a fantastic idea. The posters have a really important message that's very clear.'

- 'I really love the messages because they attract people.'

ONE BILLION RISING ACTION

One Billion Rising (OBR) happens across the world once a year on 14 February. As this was the inspiration for the Gender Respect Project, the teachers felt that it was a good example of people taking action for change for children to experience. Although the issue of gender-based violence is a sensitive one to tackle with younger children, the teachers were able to introduce the idea using PowerPoint slides developed by the group for KS2 children, dance workshops to learn the OBR dance and a senses poetry workshop, developed by creative writer in education, Ann Hamblen, to get an idea of what the demonstration is like. In the 'Ladder of Participation' (see Figure 7.5) this action would probably be lower than we would hope at rung 5: 'young people consulted and informed'. An action was suggested to the students but they were informed about the reasons and participation in the actual event was optional. It was felt that the students needed experiences of participating in this kind of action with other people to know that this was a possible course of action and how it might feel. The PowerPoint slides are available to download and adapt on the Gender Respect site.[19]

Senses poetry workshop

Preparing young students to take part in a One Billion Rising (OBR) event is a real challenge. Learning the dance that demonstrators all over the world dance on the day can be quite a hurdle in itself – helping children/young people to understand the reasons why everyone is dancing is an even greater challenge.

INITIAL PREPARATION

Procedure

1. Share with your group, in a way which you know will help them best to grasp the big picture without overfacing them, some of the content from the OBR website, explaining what One Billion Rising[20] is.

2. Search 'One Billion Rising' images on the internet for crowd scenes. Choose six clear and powerful images from around the globe to share with your students; talk briefly about each place and what is happening. Give a copy of the 'Senses' sheet to each student.

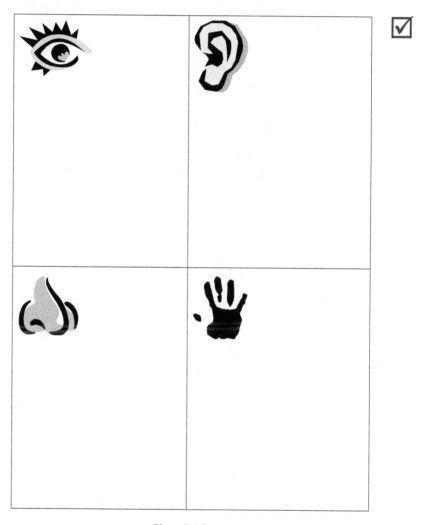

Figure 7.6 Senses

3. Show the images again, stopping for a while on each, and asking students to:

   a. Choose a person in the image with whom to identify.

   b. Use the 'Senses' sheet and complete the sentence 'I can see…' (use the eye icon box: there is no need to write the three words – the icon does this for you).

   Change image – change sense – until each student has a collection of four to five vivid sense impressions. Coach for tighter, more evocative expression as you go. Be flexible. (Short, simple responses from younger students, collected straight onto a flipchart by an adult can work brilliantly.)

   c. Each student could also choose one of the demonstrators from the One Billion Rising action, and give that person a brief voice, completing the sentence, 'I feel…' or 'I know…' and so on.

4. Extra material: some data/world figures/fact sheet statements can be interspersed as well (see the Gender Respect Project's PowerPoint presentation[21] and Amnesty International n.d.).

Amnesty Internation (n.d.) has produced a very useful set of activities, but they are aimed at 11–18-year-olds, so choose carefully for your children/young people. You might adapt some of the factual statements from Activity 1: Information Sheet, p.6, and some of the freedoms from Activity 6: Information Sheet, p.17, interspersed with your students' sense impressions. (See the box below for an example of how this might emerge, but your students should have editing/organising powers.)

5. Together, choose a group structure/order for performance (consider pattern, variety, repetition, contrast – of sound, ideas, etc.). Allocate voices – a line or lines might be read by one voice or several. Project the images you worked from behind the performers as they read the lines in their chosen order. You can make this as simple or as theatrical as you choose…just within your class or in assembly. Keep it simple – let the words and the images do the work.

This is an example of the type of material the children might produce.

ONE BILLION RISING!

Flickering of candle flames all round us in the dark
Pink streamers flying, cameras clicking
Bright patterns of all my friends' saris, close,
    shoulder to shoulder, touching
Arms raised, voices raised, fingers pointing to the sky
Dancing, clapping together as snow falls.

(Four children's sense impressions, sorted/combined into a preferred draft order. These might stay together, with others, or be interspersed with factual or other lines.)

Across the world one in three women will experience violence in her lifetime.

In England and Wales two women are killed by a male partner every two weeks (Women's Aid Federation of England 2015).

In Pakistan an average of 650 women a year are murdered in the name of 'honour' (Human Rights Commission of Pakistan 2014).

When the violence stops, women and girls will be:

Leaving their houses when they wish in Yemen.

Walking in the park at night in the United Kingdom.

Going to the gym in Saudi Arabia.

Dancing across the world.

OTHER SUGGESTIONS FOR HOW STUDENTS CAN TAKE ACTION

- Involving students in a gender audit – school walls, books, playground use, etc.
- Students interviewing each other about gender issues.
- Surveying local toy and bookshops and writing letters.
- Getting involved in national campaigns such as 'Let Toys be Toys'.

OTHER RESOURCES FOR DISCUSSING GENDER ISSUES WITH CHILDREN

'Let Toys be Toys': Lesson plan for students aged 7–9 on toys and stereotypes, www.lettoysbetoys.org.uk/toys-and-stereotypes-ks2-activity-2.

National Union of Teachers (NUT) Section, *Breaking the Mould: Challenging Gender Stereotypes.* Three booklets of guidance and lesson ideas: 'Stereotypes stop you doing stuff', 'Boys things and girls things?', 'It's child's play' (ideas to use with picture books), www.teachers.org.uk/equality/equality-matters/breaking-mould.

Stimuli for P4C: 'Boy and girl', www.youtube.com/watch?v=pF1j22x-yU8&feature=youtu.be; 'Stereo', a film about reversed gender stereotypes, written and directed by a 13-year-old girl, www.youtube.com/watch?v=ePlriYalzPY.

Teacher Guidance: Key Standards in Teaching about Body Image, www.pshe-association.org.uk/curriculum-and-resources/resources/key-standards-teaching-about-body-image, teaching materials about body image produced by the PSHE Association.

SUMMARY

This chapter has:

- discussed how explicit teaching to develop critical thinking is essential to challenge gender inequality

- introduced and explained Philosophy for Children (P4C) and provided some question plans for exploring philosophical concepts related to gender equality

- given some examples of lessons tried out in the Gender Respect Project on the themes of gender roles in a local and global context, work, sport and violence and prejudice

- given some examples of how students can be supported to take action for gender equality.

Chapter 8

CONCLUSION

KEY MESSAGES

One of the key messages of this book is that gender equality work in primary schools is needed, important and possible. It is needed because of the reality of gender inequality in society at large, as well as gender-based discrimination that still exists within schools. The big societal problems include the prevalence of gender-based violence and the still unequal access to power and resources. The root causes of these problems are gender stereotyping, underlying social norms and unequal power relationships – all of which can be challenged within schools.

Schools are not only microcosms of society at large but can also be places where change in society can be seeded and nurtured. Gender equality is possible because gender is not fixed, but learnt through the interactions that children have with others from birth onwards. Aspects of being a girl or a boy that are stereotypically limiting or lead to inequalities can be changed and challenged. Girls can succeed in mathematics and science, be in positions of power and feel confidence in their abilities. Boys can succeed in writing, feel a full range of emotions, nurture and take care of other people. Children do not have to feel limited by their assigned gender, conforming to fixed attitudes, ways of presenting themselves or behaving. Children can learn to play and work together and respect each other regardless of gender identity. In whatever ways wider society emphasises gender binaries these can be questioned by the next generation from an early stage only by bringing the issues to the attention of children and helping them to think critically and independently. So at this time in schools we have a tricky balancing act of modelling a gender-neutral environment as far as possible while enabling children to talk about the real gender inequalities that exist. Gender equality work is also challenging because the adults working in a school will all have deeply held views and assumptions about gender which they have learnt over time and live out on a day-to-day basis. Gender identity is deeply personal and therefore resistant to change. However, it is of central importance that teachers and other staff in school themselves are open to evaluating their practice and ways of being with children as their unconscious bias and expectations can have profound impacts on students' academic outcomes as well as influencing relationships in a school.

So another key message of this book is that, as with any intervention, a whole-school approach is centrally important to really embed gender equality. The hidden and taught curriculum needs to reflect gender equality and provide an essential supporting background for tackling issues of gender inequality with children through critical dialogic approaches such as Philosophy for Children (P4C).

TAKING THE WORK FORWARD

One of the aims of writing this book was to support teachers with an interest in gender equality to influence change in their schools. The first part (Chapters 1 to 4) provided evidence of why this work is not only essential in primary schools, but also how gender identities are not fixed and so change is possible. The second part of the book (Chapters 5 to 7) used the acronym ICE to suggest some ways in which gender equality can become embedded in a school, through the Implicit or hidden curriculum, the taught Curriculum and through Explicit teaching. In this concluding chapter I would like to develop the ICE analogy to offer some starting points and ways forward for whole-school change.

Imagine the school as a frozen lake – an ice rink. How do you make the first tentative steps onto the ice and progress to eventually confidently dancing with others on the lake, continuously creating your own moves?

1. Survey the lake – stand at the side and look at the lake and the skaters on it

At first glance, what are the gender equality issues in your school? Have informal conversations with other members of staff to find out whether they think there are any issues and what their levels of awareness of gender equality are. Look around at the physical environment – what are the displays and books like? Try asking a group of children for their views. Are there any large cracks in the ice or just tiny fissures?

2. Take some tentative steps onto the edge of the lake where the ice is thickest

Focus on one aspect of gender equality for a week as a mini project. For example, observe the use of language in the school (using ideas from Chapter 5 or the checklist in Appendix 2).

3. Glide around the edge, holding onto someone else's hand

- Find allies: Which other members of staff or governors are interested in this work? (Base this either on prior knowledge or the conversations you had at stage 1.) If you aren't in the senior leadership team (SLT) or the headteacher, enlist their support.

- Introduce the idea of focusing on gender equality at a staff meeting, asking members of staff to suggest areas for development. Share the results of your mini project at stage 2.

- Use the checklist in Appendix 2 to find out in more detail where the school is on different aspects of the ICE. Involve students in identifying areas for development and auditing the physical environment, for example.

4. Skate in the centre of the ice

- Set up staff meetings or training (for example, unconscious bias training) if necessary to address the areas needing development.

- Involve students by giving each class a different area to audit and make suggestions for improvement. For example, one class might look at the books in the school library; another might observe playground activities and find out whether students think that the playground is used fairly; another might notice and report on the use of spoken language in the school.

- Subject coordinators could work with others to check gender equality in the curriculum. Teachers could look at topic planning for the next term to identify where there is a gender imbalance.

- Create a series of lessons to involve students in discussions about gender equality (see Chapter 7).

- Communicate with parents/carers about the work you are doing, enlisting enthusiastic parents/careers in creating opportunities for parents/carers to discuss gender issues.

- Work with other schools to share ideas in your locality or the secondary schools that your school feeds into.

- Take care not to create cracks in the ice by doing too much at once!

5. Become an ice dancer

Work as a team to identify and create new opportunities to develop gender equality work in the school, continually reviewing and further developing practice. Be aware of the intersections of gender equality work with other equality issues, making connections and resolving problems collaboratively. Perhaps now you are at a stage where you can show your successful work to other colleagues and schools and be central in a wider discussion about gender equality in primary schools.

Appendix 1: Gender Respect Scoping Study: Images and Questions

Image description	Question
Introduction	We're researchers with a project called 'Gender Respect' which your school is part of and your teacher has given us permission to spend this time with you. We are really interested to know what it is like to be a boy or a girl here in South Yorkshire in 2014. We've got some images here to get the conversation going, then some questions about how you see the influences on you and other boys and girls your age. Display first set of images.
Sport/PE Skipping: colour image showing school playground with girls and boys skipping with individual ropes.	At games and PE are boys better at some things than girls? Why? Are girls better at some things in games and PE than boys? Why?
Women footballers: colour image showing women playing football in a stadium. Men footballers: colour image showing men playing football in a field (blurred background).	Which do you like? Why?

cont.

Image description	Question
Girls playing basketball: colour drawing (commissioned) of two girls playing basketball with a boy watching with sad face. Boys playing basketball: colour drawing (commissioned) of two boys playing basketball with girl watching with sad face. These two images are drawn to be identical except for the change from girls to boys.	What's going on in this picture? What's the boy thinking? What's going on in this picture? What's the girl thinking?
Body image Girl make-up: colour image of teenage girl in mirror putting on eye-liner. Boy hair gel: colour image (commissioned) of teenage boy in mirror putting on hair gel. Jessica Ennis (Olympic athlete): colour photograph of Jessica Ennis wearing sports clothes, showing muscles, grinning, with thumbs up. David Beckham (footballer): colour photograph of David Beckham sat in an audience watching something wearing a t-shirt showing tattooed arms.	Do you/girls at this school think a lot about their appearances? Do you/they do a lot about it? For example, clothes? Make-up? Do you/boys at this school think a lot about their appearances? Do you/they do a lot about it? For example, clothes? Hair gel? What are the influences on how young people your age look?
Relationships Cartoon boy kissing girl: colour cartoon of teenage girl and boy sitting on a bench side by side. Boy is kissing girl on cheek with red love hearts. Girl/boy friends: colour image of teenage boy and girl sitting with boy in front, both smiling.	Which do you like? Why? Can you be just a friend with a boy/girl?
Emotional expression Men crying: two full-colour close-up head/shoulders photographs of men crying (one White man and one Black man). Woman shouting: full colour close-up of woman with angry face, looking like she is shouting with her fist raised.	What do you think about these pictures? *Optional prompt*: Some people think it is not okay for men to cry or women to shout. What do you think?

Occupations and aspirations Six occupational images from 'Working Now' and 'Focus for Change' educational packs (now out of print): black and white photograph of a Rastafarian man using a sewing machine in a factory. Black and white photograph of a woman wearing hard hat fixing a roofing tile on a roof. Black and white photograph of a woman pilot standing in front of an airplane. Black and white photograph of a man in a nursery sitting down holding a toddler's hand and smiling. Colour photograph of a man in a deckchair in the garden feeding a toddler from a bowl. Black and white photograph of a woman fixing a ceiling light with a tool belt.	Which picture do you like? Why? Which picture don't you like? Why? Do you have ideas of what you would like to do when you grow up?
Direct questions Expectations and perceived unfairness.	If you were a girl/boy would you be treated differently by adults in school? Outside of school? In what way? Why do you think this is? How do your friends expect you to act? Why? Are there some things you'd like to do but can't because people say that it's only for boys/girls? If you had a magic wand and could make one wish to make it different in the way boys and girls are treated what would it be?
Thanks and confidentiality	Many thanks for sharing your ideas. You've been really helpful to the project in understanding what it is like to be a boy/girl at this time. The recording will be very useful to the research team so we are quite clear about what you said. We will ensure your name remains confidential (double check they know what this means).

Appendix 2: Gender Equality Checklist for Primary Schools

1: Beginning, 2: Developing, 3: Advanced; I: Implicit, C: Curriculum, E: Explicit

Area	Target	1	2	3
I: Expectations and attitudes	Teachers are aware of their unconscious bias.			
	Praise for ability and skills is given to all genders.			
	Behaviour management is gender-equal.			
	Boys and girls receive equal amounts of attention from teachers.			
I: Language	Pupils are referred to in a gender-neutral way.			
	Children are not unconsciously segregated by gender.			
	All staff use gender-neutral spoken and written language.			
	Sexist language and statements are challenged.			
I: Physical environment and resources	The school's principles on equality and diversity are clearly displayed.			
	There is an equal representation of genders in displays.			
	All genders are shown in a variety of roles.			
	A diverse range of families is portrayed.			
	Colour (e.g. pink and blue) is used to challenge rather than reinforce gender stereotypes.			
	Language displayed is gender-neutral			
	Classroom resources are not gender-stereotyped or segregated.			
	Play materials are gender-neutral.			
	Play areas are organised to ensure equal access by all genders.			
	Books are available that challenge stereotypes.			
	The uniform/dress code is gender-neutral.			

I: Relationships and roles	There is a culture of mutual respect across the whole school community.			
	The gender balance of roles in school is managed to be equal as far as possible.			
	Visitors that challenge stereotyped roles are invited into school.			
	All staff are aware of the school's policies on gender equality and diversity.			
	All staff have received training on gender equality and diversity.			
	Pupil roles and responsibilities are gender-balanced.			
	Girls and boys work well together in lessons.			
	All staff are aware of how they model femininities and masculinities and how they relate to different genders.			
	Visitors are made aware of gender equality policies.			
I: Playtime and playgrounds	The playground is designed to allow different kinds of activity.			
	The playground space is used equally by all genders.			
	Children who lack physical skills are coached to enable them to join in with playground activities if they want to.			
	Supervision staff are trained to teach and facilitate a variety of playground games.			
	There is a variety of attractive equipment for playground use.			
I: Extra-curricular activities	Extra-curricular activities include all genders.			
	Celebratory assemblies are gender-neutral.			
	Gender stereotypes are challenged by adults on dressing-up days.			
	School leavers and other events are portrayed in gender-neutral ways.			
C: Art and design	All students are supported in developing a full range of artistic skills.			
	Students know as many female artists as male artists.			
	Fashion and textiles art is associated with men as well as women.			
C: Computing	Computing is portrayed as creative and fun.			
	Information about women's involvement in computing is provided.			
	Computing project topics appeal to all genders without stereotyping.			

cont.

Area	Target	1	2	3
C: Design and Technology (D&T)	In Early Years, construction materials are played with equally by all genders and presented in a gender-neutral way.			
	All genders are equally comfortable with different aspects of D&T.			
	All aspects of D&T are portrayed as equally relevant to girls and boys.			
	Skills gaps are identified and extra support is given.			
	D&T tasks are described in gender-inclusive and counter-stereotyped ways.			
	The contributions of both women and men to the subject are recognised.			
	Visitors in non-stereotypical roles are invited into the school.			
C: English / language and literacy	All types of classroom talk are equally engaged in by all genders.			
	Teachers call on all genders equally to answer questions.			
	Assumptions are challenged about gendered text preferences.			
	Literature for children to read independently is reviewed regularly for gender balance and equality.			
C: Geography	Women and men are shown in non-stereotyped roles across the world.			
	Work in the home is seen as equally valuable to work outside the home.			
	Women and people of minority ethnic heritage, in positions of power and authority feature in the curriculum.			
	All genders are portrayed in active leisure pursuits.			
	All genders are involved in fieldwork and practical work on sustainability in school.			
C: History	Famous women as well as men are studied in history (other intersectionalities are also taken into account).			
	The role of women during the World Wars is studied when celebrating Remembrance Day.			
	The lives of ordinary women are studied.			
	Famous men involved in non-stereotyped roles e.g. peace building are studied.			
	Girls' and women's position in society/gender roles through time is studied.			
	The history of feminism from suffragettes until the current time is studied.			

C: Languages	There are specific purposes and real audiences for learning languages.			
	Languages are made relevant to students' own lives.			
	Personal best or collaboration is emphasised when teaching languages.			
	Students are made aware of lesson objectives to enable them to have more control over their learning.			
	Foreign languages have a high status and visible profile in the school.			
	The idea that French is only for girls is challenged.			
C: Mathematics	There are a wide range of images of different people using mathematics in different occupations and roles.			
	Girls are given experience and skills in the interpretation of 2D drawings of 3D objects and mental rotation of these images.			
	Students are given encouragement and feedback to help overcome mathematics anxiety owing to stereotype threat.			
	Group discussion and multiple strategies for understanding and problem solving are employed in mathematics.			
	Families are helped to build 'science capital' by being provided with information about the diverse ways in which pupils can use mathematics learnt in school.			
C: Music	There is no gender differentiation in who learns which musical instrument in school.			
	Singing is seen as a normal activity for all genders to participate in.			
	All genders are equally involved with different musical styles.			
	There are no differences in teachers' attitudes to girls' and boys' musical ability.			
	In percussion all genders get an equal chance to play all instruments.			
	Teachers and students know as many female classical composers as male.			
	A variety of recorded music is played from different places, times and involving women and men.			

cont.

Area	Target	1	2	3
C: PE	All genders have equal access to a full range of physical, sporting and games activities.			
	Boys' involvement in dance and gymnastics is encouraged.			
	Girls' involvement in football and other ball games is encouraged.			
	There is a focus on skills development in PE lessons. Support is offered to ensure that all children can participate in competition.			
	Invited sports coaches provide positive and non-stereotyped gender role models.			
	Students learn about famous male dancers/gymnasts and famous female footballers/rugby players, etc.			
	Teams are mixed while ensuring that girls are confident and boys don't dominate.			
	A variety of sporting and fitness opportunities are provided outside of school.			
C: PSHE and Citizenship	Boys as well as girls are helped to develop emotional literacy.			
	All students are supported in developing respectful relationships with each other including the meaning of consent from a young age.			
	All students are taught that the changes such as menstruation at puberty are natural and healthy.			
	All genders are equally involved in conflict resolution initiatives such as peer mediation or playground buddies.			
	Students know that women are involved in politics across the world.			
	Students know that equality is enshrined in the International Convention on the Rights of the Child and the Universal Declaration of Human Rights.			
C: RE	Assumptions about the role of women in different religions are challenged.			
	The role of women across all faiths is explored.			
	Religions are portrayed as diverse rather than monolithic.			
	Students are enabled to explore a diverse range of perspectives about gender and religion.			
	Women are shown to have played important roles in different religions.			
	Women as well as men from different faiths are invited in to talk about their day-to-day experiences and patterns of life.			

C: Science	The diversity of possible careers involving science is portrayed.			
	Boys' interest in biology topics and girls' interest in physics topics is actively encouraged.			
	Teachers model interest in non-gender stereotyped areas of science.			
	Teachers have the knowledge and confidence in science to support students' attainment and progression.			
	Female scientists as well as male scientists are actively portrayed.			
E: Explicit teaching	Specific opportunities for engaging students in critical discussion about gender equality are built into the curriculum.			
	Students' critical thinking about gender issues is developed.			
	Students are supported in identifying and implementing changes they wish to make individually and in the school and wider community.			

Appendix 3: A Checklist for Children's Books

	The book collection as a whole (bear in mind intersectionalities of ethnicity, disability and sexuality for all questions). These are phrased in such a way that the more ticks under 'Yes' the better.	Yes	No
1	Are all the books of good quality (text and illustrations)? (Books that are not well-written or illustrated will counteract or undermine any positive gender messages.)		
2	Is there a good balance of male and female authors from different backgrounds?		
3	Are there books with female central characters as well as male central characters (including where characters are animals or fantastical)?		
4	Are there books which show girls and boys playing and working well together?		
5	Are there books with female characters who are strong and in leadership roles as well as books with male characters showing caring and sensitivity?		
6	Is separation of books into boys' boxes and girls' boxes in classrooms or in the library avoided?		
7	Are the books which say on the cover that they are for boys or girls removed from display and only used to prompt discussion of stereotyping?		
8	Are there good quality books which actively challenge sexism and gender stereotyping?		
9	Is there a good range of non-fiction books which feature women as much as men in non-stereotyped roles?		
10	Are there biographies of famous women in different roles?		

11	Are there biographies of famous men in caring or non-violent roles?		
12	Are there books about female as well as male artists and musicians?		
13	Are there books about female scientists and mathematicians?		
14	Are there books where people are shown working together for change (as opposed to only emphasising individual heroes and heroines)?		
15	Are groups that are often invisible in society represented in non-stereotyped and diverse ways in the book collection (e.g. Gypsy, Roma or Traveller families, families with two mothers or fathers, dual-heritage families, transgender adults and children, families who practice Islam, homeless families, multi-generational families, single-parent and step-parent families, children in foster care or adopted, disabled adults or children, etc.)?		

Checking individual books for sexism		
		Yes	No
1	Is the book of good quality (text and illustrations)? (Books that are not well-written or illustrated will counteract or undermine any positive gender messages.)		
2	Are gender stereotypes avoided (e.g. female characters in caring roles or as evil witches; male characters in active dominant roles, saving female characters)?		
3	Are the achievements of female characters based on their own initiative and intelligence rather than being reliant on their appearance or relationship with male characters?		
4	Are family roles and relationships depicted in non-stereotyped ways?		
5	Is sexist language that excludes or demeans girls or women avoided?		
6	Are pronouns used correctly (rather than using the male pronoun to refer to all genders)?		
7	Is gender-neutral language used (e.g. firefighter rather than fireman)?		
8	Are female characters depicted in the foreground of illustrations as much as male characters?		

Appendix 4: Recommended Books for Children

In this list of recommended books I have chosen good quality books that relate to gender equality in different ways. Most of the books challenge gender stereotyping in one way or another, whether by offering alternative roles, occupations or behaviour. Some of the fiction books are chosen because of the strong central female character(s); many of them also reflect ethnic diversity or are set in countries of the Global South. Some of the books portray positive friendships between girls and boys. Biographies of famous women are included. It was harder to find books that portrayed alternative ways to be a boy or non-binary gender identities in general, but these are included where they have been found. The recommended age groups are, of course, approximate. There is a huge list of 'girl-empowering' books (and other media) on the American 'A Mighty Girl' website,[1] and on the Letterbox Library website[2] in the UK.

FICTION
For ages five to seven

Ada Twist Scientist, Andrea Beaty and David Roberts, Harry N. Abrams

> Ada Twist's head is full of questions. Like her classmates Iggy and Rosie, Ada has always been endlessly curious. But when her fact-finding missions and elaborate scientific experiments go too far, her frazzled parents banish her to the Thinking Chair. Will all that thinking change Ada's mind? Great story with central female, Black character.

And Tango Makes Three, Justin Richardson, Little Simon

> Based on a true story that happened in Central Park Zoo, New York, about two male penguins who adopt an egg, this heart-warming tale shows that all that is needed to make a family is love. Suitable as a stimulus for a philosophical enquiry.

Big Bob, Little Bob, James Howe, Walker Books

Big Bob and Little Bob have the same name but like to play and do very different things. Big Bob likes to play with trucks and Little Bob likes to play with dolls. When a new girl moves into the neighborhood who also prefers trucks to dolls they realise that they can all play together and all choose what they like regardless of whether they are a boy or a girl.

Dogs Don't Do Ballet, Anna Kemp and Sara Ogilvie, Simon & Schuster Children's UK

Biff is not like ordinary dogs – instead of scratching his fleas and drinking out of the toilet, he likes the moonlight, music and walking on his tiptoes. In fact, Biff doesn't even think he's a dog; he thinks he is a ballerina.

How the Library Saved Rapunzel, Wendy Meddour, Frances Lincoln Children's Books

Refreshing new take on traditional Rapunzel story set in a city high rise. In the end it's a new job at the library that gets Rapunzel down from her tower (after she has fixed the lift). Nicely challenges some gender stereotypes.

In a Minute, Tony Bradman and Eileen Browne, Frances Lincoln Children's Books

Companion to *Through my Window* and *Wait and See*, a story of a child's everyday frustration when she has to wait for adults to have their various conversations on the way to the playground. This picture book is one of the few representing a dual-heritage family and also challenges gender stereotypes.

Izzy Gizmo, Pip Jones and Sara Ogilvie, Simon & Schuster Children's UK

Izzy Gizmo's inventions are marvellous, magnificent…and often malfunction. When she rescues an injured crow, her imagination is tested to its limit. Can she invent some new wings? Or is her new friend destined to live as a crow who can't fly? Full of fun illustrations, this story has a central Black girl who is good at science and technology.

Made by Raffi, Craig Pomranz and Margaret Chamberlain, Frances Lincoln Children's Books

Raffi feels different from the other children at school – he doesn't like noisy games, and sometimes he gets teased. But when Raffi discovers knitting and sewing, everything changes… and everyone wants to have something that is – Made By Raffi.

Not All Princesses Dress in Pink, Jane Yolen, Simon & Schuster Children's Publishing

These princesses dig in the dirt, kick footballs and splash in muddy puddles, all in their sparkly crowns! A funny, lively and colourfully illustrated catalogue of scenarios which counter gender stereotypes.

Pass it Polly, Sarah Garland, Frances Lincoln Children's Books

Polly and Nisha are the only girls who want to play in the school football team. But football turns out to be harder than it looks. With help from Nisha's grandpa and a lot of determination, they are soon dribbling, tackling and scoring goals and they go on to help their team win the match. A reprint of a classic picture book which promotes gender and race equality.

Princess Pigsty, Cornelia Funke, Kerstin Meyer and Chantal Wright, Scholastic US

Originally published in Germany, this book is about a little princess who rebels against the cushy life she is expected to lead – it is so boring. Unfortunately for her father, she really enjoys all the punishments he gives her. Eventually she wins him round.

Red Rockets and Rainbow Jelly, Sue Heap and Nick Sharratt, Picture Puffin Books

Nick likes yellow socks, Sue likes purple hair. Nick likes green aliens, Sue likes red dogs, but the one thing they both like is…each other! Brightly illustrated story about girls and boys getting along.

Storm Whale, Sarah Brennan and Jane Tanner, Old Barn Books

'Bleak was the day and the wind whipped down When I and my sisters walked to town…' So begins the story of three sisters who find a whale stranded on a windswept beach and try to save it. With a powerful poetic text and beautiful illustrations full of life and movement, this book celebrates the majesty and vulnerability of nature and our place in it while portraying three central girl characters.

Super Daisy and the Peril of Planet Pea, Kes Gray and Nick Sharratt, Red Fox Picture Books

One of the series of stories about the much-loved character, Daisy, of *Eat Your Peas* fame. In this one there's going to be a disastrous collision with Planet Pea unless 'Super Daisy' can come to the rescue. Great story for stimulating girls' superhero play.

The Big Brother, Stephanie Dragg and Alan Clarke, O'Brien Press

This book is designed for young readers who are just ready to begin reading a longer book. This is a slim paperback with supportive line drawings on each page. Dara's Mum is going to have a new baby so Dara will soon be a big brother. What does a big brother do with a little baby? Along with Dara's preparations to become a big brother the adults learn, too.

The Boy Who Grew Flowers, Jen Wojtowicz, Barefoot Books Ltd.

Rink is a very unusual boy who grows beautiful flowers all over his body whenever the moon is full. In town and at school, Rink and his family are treated as outcasts although no one knows his strange botanical secret. But one day a new girl arrives at school, and Rink discovers she has some unique qualities of her own. Using humour and metaphor to promote acceptance, this story would be useful in promoting discussion about diversity.

The Cow Who Climbed a Tree, Gemma Merino, Macmillan Children's Books

Tina isn't like other cows. She loves to explore and discover and dream. Can she show her sisters that there is more to life than chewing grass?

The Great Googly Moogly, Courtney Dicmas, Child's Play (International) Ltd.

Nobody has ever been able to catch the Great Googly Moogly – a giant and terrifying fish of legend. But Stella aims to do just that. Armed with fishing gear and different baits, she sets out every day to realise her dream, whatever the weather. But what will she do if she succeeds?

The Paper Bag Princess, Robert Munsch and Michael Martchenko, Annick Press

73rd printing of a classic alternative fairy tale. When a dragon burns down her castle and all her clothes and carries off the prince Elizabeth is due to marry she is determined to get him back and stand up to the dragon. She cleverly tricks the dragon and finds the prince, who says she isn't a real princess as she's only wearing a paper bag. Elizabeth sends him packing and presumably lives happily ever after…

Through My Window, Tony Bradman and Eileen Browne, Frances Lincoln Children's Books

When Jo has to stay in bed for a day, her dad looks after her and her mum promises to bring a special present home from work. While Jo waits she looks out of her window at all the goings-on in the street, and gets more and more excited about what her mum's special surprise will be… This picture book is one of the few representing a dual-heritage family as well as challenging gender stereotypes.

William's Doll, Charlotte Zolotow, Harper & Row

William wants a doll – to hug, to feed, to tuck in, and kiss goodnight. 'Don't be a creep', says his brother. 'Sissy, sissy', chants the boy next door. His father buys him trains and a basketball, but not the doll that William really wants. Then one day, someone comes along who understands why William should have his doll.

10,000 Dresses, Marcus Ewert and Rex Ray, Seven Stories Press

Every night, Bailey dreams about magical dresses: dresses made of crystals and rainbows, dresses made of flowers… But when Bailey's awake no one wants to hear about his dreams and they tell him that boys don't wear dresses. Then Bailey meets Laurel, an older girl who is inspired by Bailey's imagination and courage. In friendship, the two of them begin making dresses together.

For ages seven to eleven

An Angel Just Like Me, Mary Hoffmann, Frances Lincoln Children's Books

This story is about a little boy who can't understand why there aren't any Black angels like him. His friend, Carl, who is an artist, solves his problem by making him an angel that looks just like him. Great story for tackling issues around race and gender with young children. Would also be a useful stimulus for Philosophy for Children (P4C).

Azzi in Between, Sarah Garland, Frances Lincoln Children's Books

Endorsed by Amnesty International, this story by well-loved children's author Sarah Garland draws on her own experiences among refugee families to tell the story of a little girl having to escape from her own country and come to Britain.

Bill's New Frock, Anne Fine, Egmont

One day, Bill wakes up to find he's a girl. And worse, his mum makes him wear a pink frock to school. Bill discovers that everything is very different for girls. Now a classic, this is a funny and thought-provoking book.

Butterfly Park, Elly Mackay, Running Press Kids

A young girl discovers a vacant park next door to her new house that is intended for butterflies, but when she has trouble getting butterflies to stay there, her new neighbours help her plant flowers to attract them. The beautiful, paper-cut illustrations would inspire artwork, and the story, with its themes of sustainability, community and friendship, would make it an ideal stimulus for philosophical enquiry.

Football Star, Mina Javaherbin, Walker Books

When Paulo becomes a football star, he'll be famous. Crowds will cheer his name – and his mother won't have to work so hard. Until then, Paulo has his little sister Maria, who teaches him mathematics, while he teaches her football moves. Will his teammates ever break the rules and let a girl play with them? A great book for challenging gender stereotypes through a global approach.

Four Feet Two Sandals, Karen Lynn Williams and Khadra Mohammed, Eerdmans Books for Young Readers

Moving story about the friendship of two girls living in an Afghan refugee camp in Pakistan.

Girl Underground, Morris Gleitzman, Puffin

Sequel to *Boy Overboard*, in this book smart Bridget teams up with a minister's son to expose Australia's treatment of refugees and rescue Jamal and Bibi from a desert detention centre.

Horace and Morris but mostly Dolores, James Howe, Aladdin Paperbacks

Horace, Morris and Dolores have been friends forever. They do everything together – from sailing the Seven Sewers to climbing Mount Ever-Rust. But one day Horace and Morris join the Mega-Mice (no girls allowed) and Dolores joins the Cheese Puffs (no boys allowed). Is this the end? Or will Horace and Morris but mostly Dolores find a way to save the day, and their friendship? Winner of a number of awards, 'a spirited tribute to friendship and individuality'.

Masha and the Bear, Lari Don, Barefoot Books

It's easy to get lost in the forest. Little Masha lives on the edge of a big forest in Russia. But one day she is so busy picking berries that she goes too far and loses her way. A re-told traditional Russian tale where a girl outwits a bear and forces him to do his own cooking and cleaning.

Mia's Story, Michael Foreman, Walker Books

Inspiring story based on Foreman's experience of meeting the villagers of Campamento San Francisco in the Chilean Andes. The village used to be surrounded by farmland but as the nearby city grew, all the villagers could harvest was the rubbish that the city threw away. The central character, a little girl called Mia, makes a wonderful discovery when her dog goes missing in the mountains, which changes their lives forever. The beautiful illustrations convey the contrasts between the drab village, the whiteness of the mountains and the vibrancy of the city.

Peace Maker, Malorie Blackman, Barrington Stokes

A thrilling futuristic tale of adventure, danger and personal responsibility from *Noughts and Crosses* bestseller Malorie Blackman. Inclusive and thought-provoking, this great novel with a central girl character invites the reader to engage with questions of human nature and the necessity of violence. Particularly suitable for struggling, reluctant and dyslexic readers aged eight plus.

Piggybook, Anthony Browne, Walker Books

Mr Piggott and his two sons behave like pigs to poor Mrs Piggott until, finally, she walks out. Left to fend for themselves, the male Piggotts undergo some curious changes! A hard-hitting book wonderfully illustrated, as always, by Anthony Browne, which challenges sexism.

Rosie Revere, Engineer, Andrea Beaty and David Roberts, Abrams Books for Young Readers

Based on the fictional character of Rosie the Riveter who represented all the women who were involved in war work in the US during the Second World War, this witty picture book shows that girls can be engineers and inventors and everyone should pursue their passion and persevere in the face of failure.

Something Beautiful, Sharon Dennis Wyeth, Random House USA Children's Books

Wonderful story about an inner-city girl who faces graffiti and rubbish outside her flat every morning. When her teacher writes the word 'beautiful' on the blackboard, she decides to look for something beautiful in her neighbourhood. Many different people show her the things which they find beautiful and she decides that beautiful means 'something that when you have it, your heart is happy'. At the end of the book she decides to clean up the rubbish herself and get rid of the graffiti.

The Butterfly Heart, Paula Leyden, Walker Books

Bul-Boo and Madillo are powerless to save their friend Winifred from a terrifying fate and time is slipping away. In desperation they call upon Ifwafwa, the snake man. But although the old man is wise, he is slow and the girls become impatient. Will he strike before it is too late? This sensitively written story is about the human rights abuses suffered by women and girls across the world.

The Girl with the Brave Heart, Rita Jahanforuz, Barefoot Books

Shiraz does not think of herself as being brave, but when she drops her ball of red wool from the balcony, she knows she will need all of her courage if she is to retrieve it. For the ball of wool has landed in a neighbour's garden, and the person who owns the garden is very unusual. A beautifully illustrated folk tale from Tehran which would be a good stimulus for philosophical enquiry.

The Moon Dragons, Dyan Sheldon and Gary Blythe, Andersen Press

This enchanting story tells of Alina, a young peasant girl who succeeds where others have failed in finding the moon dragons high up on the mountainside. She turns down a room full of gold to protect them.

The Green Bicycle, Haifaa al-Mansour, Puffin

Wadjda has one simple wish – to ride her very own bicycle in a race with her friend Abdullah. But in Saudi Arabia it is considered improper for girls to ride bikes, and her parents forbid her from having one. Sick of playing by the rules, Wadjda invents different schemes to make money to buy the bike herself. Based on the award-winning film *Wadjda*.

The Secret of Nightingale Woods, Lucy Strange, Chicken House

In 1919 Henry moves to the countryside with her family, scarred by her brother's untimely death. Her only friends are characters from her favourite – until, one day, she wanders into the woods and meets Moth, a striking witchlike woman. Together they form a bond that could help Henry save her family and overcome her grief.

The Wolf Wilder, Katherine Rundell, Bloomsbury Children's Books

Feodora's mother is a wolf wilder, and Feo is a wolf wilder in training. A wolf wilder is the opposite of an animal tamer: it is a person who teaches tamed animals to fend for themselves, and to fight and to run, and to be wary of humans. When the murderous hostility of the Russian Army threatens her very existence, Feo is left with no option but to go on the run. What follows is a story of revolution, adventure and standing up for the things you love. And, of course, wolves. A compelling story with male and female characters that defy gender stereotypes.

When the Bees Fly Home, Andrea Cheng, Tilbury House

A sensitive story about an artistic boy who, while not as physically strong as the other men in his family, is just as gifted.

NON-FICTION
For ages five to seven

Amelia Earhart, Isabel Sanchez Vegara and Maria Diamantes, Frances Lincoln Children's Books

A simple and boldly illustrated version of the biography of Amelia Earhart, the famous early 20th century pilot.

Malala, a Brave Girl from Pakistan / Iqbal, a Brave Boy from Pakistan, Jeanette Winter, Simon & Schuster Children's

Two picture books in one, connecting in the middle, tell the true stories of Malala Yousafzai, Nobel Peace Prize Winner and Iqbal Masih, who was shot for speaking out against child labour.

The Barefoot Book of Children, Tessa Strickland, Barefoot Books

Fantastic book with detailed and vibrant illustrations of children doing everyday things around the world. The illustrators have taken great care to be as inclusive as possible, including making sure there is no gender stereotyping. A section at the back gives factual information about the pictures.

The Voyage of Mae Jemison, Susan Canizares and Samantha Berger, Scholastic

Photographic book with simple text about the Black woman astronaut, Mae Jemison. The biography at the back of the book would be suitable for older pupils.

Wangari's Trees for Peace, Jeanette Winter, Harcourt Children's Books

A version of the inspiring story of Kenyan Nobel Peace Prize Winner, Wangari Maathai, for younger children. This story could be used within a theme of forests and sustainability or to show that people in Africa can and do take control of their own lives. As Wangari Maathai said, 'I always felt that our work was not simply about planting trees. It was about inspiring people to take charge of their environment, the system that governed them, their lives and their future.'

What Are You Playing At?, Marie-Sabine Roger and Anne Sol, Alanna Books

A sturdy lift-the-flap book for young children which challenges stereotypes of what boys and girls can do, with photographs of adult women and men engaged in those activities. Great for encouraging discussions around gender roles.

When I Grow Up, Benjamin Zephaniah, Frances Lincoln Children's Books

Maggie is a space scientist! Then there's Michelle the vet, Ness the pilot and Bubblz the mathematical clown to name but a few of the fantastic range of jobs for the 21st century. Benjamin Zephaniah's poetry gets to the heart of what all these people do for a living. Each poem is complemented by superb photographs and a biography of each of these people going about their jobs.

Who Are You? The Kid's Guide to Gender Identity, Brook Pessin-Whedbee and Naomi Bardoff, Jessica Kingsley Publishers

An introduction to gender for ages three plus, with straightforward language for talking about how we experience gender: our body, our expression and our gender identity. Includes an interactive wheel and a guide for adults.

For ages seven to eleven

Black Women Scientists and Inventors Volume 1, Michael Williams and Djehuti Ankh Kheru, BIS Publications

Book of historical and contemporary Black women scientists and inventors. A page of information with photographs on each is accompanied by questions based on the text and ideas for science experiments.

Emmeline Pankhurst, Lisbeth Kaiser, Frances Lincoln Children's Books

As a child, Emmeline Pankhurst was inspired by books about heroes who fought for others. She dedicated her life to fighting for women's voting rights and, with hard work and great bravery, led a remarkable movement that changed the world. This story of her incredible life features a facts and photos section at the back.

Frida Kahlo and the Bravest Girl in the World, Laurence Anholt, Barron's Educational Series

Told through the perspective of Mariana, a real child who knew Frida Kahlo, the famous Mexican artist, this wonderful story features seven paintings by the artist and is a good introduction to her life and work for young readers.

Goodnight Stories for Rebel Girls 1 and 2, Elena Favilli and Francesca Cavallo, Particular Books

Each of these beautifully illustrated books tells the stories of 100 remarkable women, from Nefertiti to Michelle Obama.

I am Malala, Malala Yousafzai and Christina Lamb, Phoenix

Inspiring memoir by Nobel Peace Prize Winner, Malala Yousafzai, who fought for her right to education and continues to speak up for girls' rights around the world.

Liberté: The Life of Noor Inayat Khan, Chorlton CofE Primary School, Ahmed Iqbal Ullah Race Relations Archive

Biography of a famous Muslim woman who became a spy in the Second World War, written and illustrated by Year 6 pupils of a primary school in Manchester.

Peaceful Heroes, Jonah Winter, Arthur A. Levine Books

A tribute to 14 women and men who have risked their lives to help others and make the world a better place. Includes Corrie ten Boom, Abdul Ghaffar Khan, Oscar Romero, Paul Rusesbagina and Marla Ruzicka as well as Gandhi, Sojourner Truth and Martin Luther King.

Rosa Parks, Lisbeth Kaiser, Frances Lincoln Children's Books

Rosa Parks grew up in Alabama, where she learned to stand up for herself at an early age. Rosa went on to become a civil rights activist whose courage and dignity sparked the movement that ended segregation. She never stopped working for equal rights. This inspiring story of her life features a facts and photos section at the back.

Sea Queens: Women Pirates Around the World, Jane Yolen, Charlesbridge

This book charts the lives of some of the most famous – and infamous – woman pirates including the most powerful pirate of all time, Madame Ching.

The Librarian of Basra, Jeanette Winter, Harcourt, Inc.

Inspiring picture book account of the true story of Alia Muhammad Baker, chief librarian of Basra's Central Library, who managed to resource 70 per cent of the library's collection before the library burned in the Iraq war nine days later. Could be used as a stimulus for a philosophical enquiry.

We Are All Born Free, Amnesty International, Frances Lincoln Children's Books

Published to coincide with the 60th anniversary of the Declaration of Human Rights, in association with Amnesty International. A beautiful collection of illustrations celebrating each right, drawn by internationally renowned artists.

Women in Science: 50 Fearless Pioneers Who Changed the World, Rachel Ignotovsky, Wren and Rook

A celebration of trailblazing women in STEM careers – from the well known, such as Marie Curie, to the relatively unknown Katherine Johnson – this is a wonderfully illustrated and inspiring book.

Women in Sport: 50 Fearless Athletes Who Played to Win, Rachel Ignotovsky, Wren and Rook

Celebrates the achievements of 50 female athletes from the 1800s to the present day.

13 Women Artists Children Should Know, Bettina Schuemann, Prestel

Book with large colour pictures of paintings by famous women artists. Most of the artists are European (or Mexican, Frida Kahlo), but the book is a good introduction to women artists from different periods and balances the more common focus on male artists.

100 Women Who Made History, Stella Caldwell, Dorling Kindersley Children

Attractive, lively and accessible, this book of important women through history looks at women involved in creative arts, science, campaigning, politics, business and sport.

References

American Foundation for Suicide Prevention (2017) *'Suicide Statistics.'* Accessed on 20/5/17 at www.afsp.org/about-suicide/suicide-statistics.

Amnesty International (n.d.) *Human Rights Education Activities for Use in Teaching Personal, Social, Health and Economic Education (PSHE), Citizenship and English for Ages 11–18.* Accessed on 9/2/18 at www.amnesty.org.uk/files/lesson_2_3.pdf.

Amnesty International (2008) *We Are All Born Free.* London: Frances Lincoln.

Apostolova, V. and Cracknell, R. (2017) *Women in Parliament and Government.* House of Commons Library Briefing Paper Number SN01250. Accessed on 3/12/17 at http://researchbriefings.parliament.uk/ResearchBriefing/Summary/SN01250.

Apostolova, V., Baker, C. and Cracknell, R. (2017) 'Women in Public Life, the Professions and the Boardroom.' (Open Parliament License.) Accessed on 8/2/18 at http://researchbriefings.parliament.uk/ResearchBriefing/Summary/SN05170#fullreport.

APPG (All-Party Parliamentary Group) on body image (2012) 'Reflections on body image.' Accessed on 29/8/17 at http://ymca-central-assets.s3-eu-west-1.amazonaws.com/s3fs-public/APPG-Reflections-on-body-image.pdf.

ASPIRES (2013) *Young People's Science and Career Aspirations Age 10–14 (Final Report).* London: Kings College.

Ball, R. and Millar, J. (2017) *The Gender Agenda: A First-Hand Account of How Girls and Boys Are Treated Differently.* London and Philadelphia, PA: Jessica Kingsley Publishers.

BBC (2017) 'Rio Ferdinand: My kids would not talk about grief.' 27 March. Accessed on 29/5/17 at www.bbc.co.uk/news/uk-39392101.

BBC Radio 4 (2017) 'The everyday effect of unconscious bias.' 17 May. Accessed on 18/8/17 at www.bbc.co.uk/programmes/b08q60pr.

Bramley, T., Vidal Rodeiro, C.L. and Vitello, S. (2015) *Gender Differences in GCSE.* Cambridge Assessment Research Report. Cambridge: Cambridge Assessment.

Browne, N. (2004) *Gender Equity in the Early Years.* Maidenhead: Open University Press.

Brizendine, L. (2007) *The Female Brain.* London: Bantam Press.

Campaign for Science and Engineering (2014) *Improving Diversity in STEM.* Accessed on 15/8/17 at www.sciencecampaign.org.uk/resource/ImprovingDiversityinSTEM2014.html.

Chadha, G. (dir.) (2002) *Bend it Like Beckham.* Bend It Films.

Cimpian, J., Lubienski, S., Timmer, J., Makowski, M. and Miller, E. (2016) 'Have gender gaps in math closed? Achievement, teacher perceptions, and learning behaviors across two ECLS-K cohorts.' *AERA Open 2,* 4, 1–19.

Claxton, G. (2002) *Building Learning Power.* London: TLO Limited.

Connell, R.W. (1995) *Masculinities.* Sydney: Allen & Unwin.

Craven, R.G., Marsh, H.W. and Debus, R.L. (1991) 'Effects of internally focused feedback and attributional feedback on enhancement of academic self-concept.' *Journal of Educational Psychology 83,* 1, 17–27.

CSW57 (Commission on the Status of Women 57) (2013) *Agreed Conclusions on the Elimination and Prevention of All Forms of Violence Against Women and Girls.* Accessed on 13/5/17 at www.un.org/womenwatch/daw/csw/csw57/CSW57_Agreed_Conclusions_(CSW_report_excerpt).pdf.

Daldry, S. (dir.) (2000) *Billy Elliot.* Universal Pictures.

Davies, B. (2002) *Frogs and Snails and Feminist Tales.* Revised edn. New York: Hampton Press.

Davies, C. (2015) 'Number of suicides in UK increases, with male rate highest since 2001.' *The Guardian,* 19 February. Accessed on 20/5/17 at www.theguardian.com/society/2015/feb/19/number-of-suicides-uk-increases-2013-male-rate-highest-2001.

DCSF (Department for Children, Schools and Families) (2009) *Gender Issues in Schools – What Works to Improve Achievement for Boys and Girls.* Accessed on 5/5/17 at http://dera.ioe.ac.uk/9094/1/00601-2009BKT-EN.pdf.

DECSY (Development Education Centre South Yorkshire) (2016) Gender Respect Pupil Conference film. Accessed on 13/5/17 at https://vimeo.com/157211321.

DfE (Department for Education) (2013) *The National Curriculum in England Key Stages 1 and 2 Framework Document.* Accessed on 10/8/17 at www.gov.uk/government/publications/national-curriculum-in-england-framework-for-key-stages-1-to-4.

DfE (2017) *Schools to Teach 21st Century Relationships and Sex Education.* Accessed on 5/5/17 at www.gov.uk/government/news/schools-to-teach-21st-century-relationships-and-sex-education.

Doherr, E. (2000) 'The demonstration of cognitive abilities central to cognitive behavioural therapy in young people: Examining the influence of age and teaching method on degree of ability.' Unpublished clinical psychology doctoral dissertation, University of East Anglia.

Durkin, K. (1985) *Television, Sex Roles, and Children.* Milton Keynes: Open University Press.

Dweck, C. (2006) *Mindset: The New Psychology of Success.* New York: Ballantine Books.

Dweck, C. (2008) 'Brainology.' Accessed on 31/5/17 at www.nais.org/magazine/independent-school/winter-2008/brainology.

End Violence Against Women (2017) 'YouGov poll exposes high levels sexual harassment in schools.' Accessed on 29/5/17 at www.endviolenceagainstwomen.org.uk/yougov-poll-exposes-high-levels-sexual-harassment-in-schools.

Epstein, D., Kehily, M., Mac an Ghaill, M. and Redman, P. (2001) 'Boys and girls come out to play: Making masculinities and femininities in school playgrounds.' *Men and Masculinities 4,* 2, 158–172.

Equality and Human Rights Commission (Last updated 16 May 2016) 'Why teach equality and human rights.' Accessed on 9/4/17 at www.equalityhumanrights.com/en/secondary-education-resources/useful-information/why-teach-equality-and-human-rights.

Evaldsson, A.C. (2003) 'Throwing like a girl? Situating gender differences in physicality across game contexts.' *Childhood 10,* 4, 475–497.

Fawcett Society, The (2017a) 'Equal pay day briefing 2017.' Accessed on 2/3/18 at www.fawcettsociety.org.uk/equal-pay-day-2017-briefing.

Fawcett Society, The (2017b) 'Close the gender pay gap.' Accessed on 29/8/17 at www.fawcettsociety.org.uk/close-gender-pay-gap.

Fine, C. (2010) *Delusions of Gender: The Real Science Behind Sex Differences.* London: Icon Books.

Fine, C. (2017) *Testosterone Rex.* London: Icon Books.

Francis, B. (1998) *Power Plays: Primary School Children's Constructions of Gender, Power, and Adult Work.* Stoke on Trent: Trentham Books.

Fuller, A. and Unwin, L. (2013) *Gender Segregation and Apprenticeship and the Raising of the Participation Age in England: Are Young Women at a Disadvantage?* London: Centre for Learning and Life Chances in Knowledge Economies and Societies, Institute of Education, University of London. Accessed on 28/5/17 at www.llakes.ac.uk/sites/default/files/44.%20Fuller%20and%20Unwin.pdf.

Furness, H. (2017) 'Prince Harry: I sought counselling after 20 years of not thinking about the death of my mother, Diana, and two years of total chaos in my life.' *The Telegraph,* 19 April. Accessed on 29/5/17 at www.telegraph.co.uk/news/2017/04/16/prince-harry-sought-counselling-death-mother-led-two-years-total.

Gender Respect Project blog (2014) Accessed on 13/3/18 at https://genderrespect2013.wordpress.com/2014/11/13/teacher-blog-stephen-adults-modelling-respect-for-each-other-is-so-important.

GHO (Global Health Observatory) (2010) *Violence Against Women.* Accessed on 28/3/14 at www. who.int/gho/women_and_health/violence/en/.

Girlguiding (2016) 'Girls' Attitudes Survey.' Accessed on 19/4/17 at www.girlguiding.org.uk/ globalassets/docs-and-resources/research-and-campaigns/girls-attitudes-survey-2016.pdf.

Gray, J. (2008) *Why Mars and Venus Collide.* London: HarperCollins.

Griffin, H. (2014) 'The Implementation of Philosophy for Children within the Xiehe Education Organisation.' In T. Higginbottom (ed.) *Developing Global Schools in China: East Meets West.* Leek: Lifeworlds Learning.

Hanlon, D. (1992) 'Religious Education.' In K. Myers (ed.) *Genderwatch: After the ERA.* Cambridge: Cambridge University Press.

Hart, R. (1992) *Children's Participation from Tokenism to Citizenship.* Florence: UNICEF Innocenti Research Centre.

Health and Social Care Information Centre (2016) 'Provisional Monthly Hospital Episode Statistics for Admitted Patient Care, Outpatients and Accident Emergency Data – April 2015 to January 2016.' Accessed on 22/12/17 at http://content.digital.nhs.uk/catalogue/PUB20298/prov-mont-hes-admi-outp-ae-April%202015%20to%20January%202016-toi-rep.pdf.

HM Government (2016) 'Ending Violence against Women and Girls Strategy 2016–2020.' Accessed on 19/5/17 at www.gov.uk/government/uploads/system/uploads/attachment_data/file/522166/VAWG_Strategy_FINAL_PUBLICATION_MASTER_vRB.PDF.

House of Commons, Women and Equalities Committee (2016) 'Sexual Harassment and Violence in Schools, Third Report of Session 2016–2017 HC 91.' Accessed on 17/4/17 at www. publications.parliament.uk/pa/cm201617/cmselect/cmwomeq/91/91.pdf.

House of Commons International Development Committee (2016) 'UK Implementation of the Sustainable Development Goals. First Report of Session 2016–2017, HC103.' Accessed on 5/5/17 at www.publications.parliament.uk/pa/cm201617/cmselect/cmintdev/103/103.pdf.

Horvath, M.A.H., Alys, L., Massey, K., Pina, A., Scally, M. and Adler, J.R. (2011) *'Basically…Porn is Everywhere': A Rapid Evidence Assessment on the Effect that Access and Exposure to Pornography has on Children and Young People.* Office of the Children's Commissioner. Accessed on 29/5/17 at www. mdx.ac.uk/__data/assets/pdf_file/0026/48545/BasicallyporniseverywhereReport.pdf.

Human Rights Commission of Pakistan (2014) 'Honor crimes.' Accessed on 13/13/18 at http:// hrcpmonitor.org/search/?id=5.

Hutchinson, J., Rolfe, H., Moore, N., Bysshe, S. and Bentley, K. (2011) *All Things Being Equal? Equality and Diversity in Careers Education, Information, Advice and Guidance.* Manchester: Equality and Human Rights Commission. Accessed on 28/5/17 at https://derby.openrepository.com/ derby/handle/10545/197211.

Institute of Physics (2013) *Closing Doors: Exploring Gender and Subject Choice in School.* London: Institute of Physics. Accessed on 15/4/17 at www.iop.org/education/teacher/support/girls_physics/ closing-doors/page_62076.html.

Institute of Physics (2015) *Opening Doors: A Guide to Good Practice in Countering Stereotyping in Schools.* London: Institute of Physics. Accessed on 19/5/17 at www.iop.org/publications/iop/2015/ page_66430.html.

Interparliamentary Union (2017) 'Women in National Parliaments.' Accessed on 3/12/17 at http:// archive.ipu.org/wmn-e/classif.htm.

Jascz, M. (2015) 'Why we should stop calling women "guys".' *Huffington Post,* 5 September. Accessed on 8/8/17 at www.huffingtonpost.com/michael-jascz/why-we-should-stop-callin_b_8091436. html.

Johns, M., Schmader, T. and Martens, A. (2005) 'Knowing is half the battle: Teaching stereotype threat as a means of improving women's math performance.' *Psychological Science 16,* 3, 175–179.

Joint Council for Qualifications (2017) 'GCSE and A-level examination results 2017.' Accessed on 6/10/17 at www.jcq.org.uk/examination-results/gcses/2017 and www.jcq.org.uk/ examination-results/a-levels/2017.

Jones, B. (2017) 'Boosting boys' motivation in MFL.' Accessed on 6/10/17 at www.all-languages. org.uk/wp-content/uploads/2017/01/Boosting-Boys-Motivation.pdf.

Jones, S. and Myhill, D. (2004) 'Seeing things differently: Teachers' constructions of underachievement.' *Gender and Education 16,* 4, 531–546.

Kamins, M.L. and Dweck, C. (1999) 'Person versus process praise and criticism: Implications for contingent self-worth and coping.' *Developmental Psychology 35*, 3, 835–847.

Kane, E.W. (2006) '"No way my boys are going to be like that!" Parents' responses to children's gender nonconformity.' *Gender and Society 20*, 149–176.

Kennedy, M. (2017) 'Prince Harry grief revelations draw praise from mental health experts.' *The Guardian*, 17 April. Accessed on 29/5/17 at www.theguardian.com/society/2017/apr/17/prince-harry-grief-revelations-praise-mental-health-experts.

Kenway, J. and Fitzclarence, L. (1997) 'Masculinity, Violence and Schooling.' In M. Arnot and M. Mac an Ghaill (eds) *The Routledge Falmer Reader in Gender and Education* (2006). London: Routledge.

Kimmel, M.S. (2008) *The Gendered Society*. Oxford: Oxford University Press.

Lamb, L.M., Bigler, L.S., Liben, L.S. and Green, V.A. (2009) 'Teaching children to confront peers' sexist remarks: Implications for theories of gender development and educational practice.' *Sex Roles 61*, 361–382.

Levinson, D. (1989) *Family Violence in Cross-Cultural Perspective*. London: Sage Publications.

Liben, L.S., Bigler, R. and Krogh, H. (2001) 'Pink and blue collar jobs: Children's judgments of job status and job aspirations in relation to sex of worker.' *Journal of Experimental Child Psychology 79*, 358.

Lindon, J. (2006) *Equality in Early Childhood*. London: Hodder Arnold.

MacNaughton, G. (2000) *Rethinking Gender in Early Childhood Education*. London: Paul Chapman.

Martin, B. (2011) *Children at Play: Learning Gender in the Early Years*. Stoke on Trent: Trentham Books Ltd.

Maynard, T. (2002) *Boys and Literacy: Exploring the Issues*. London: Routledge Falmer.

McDonald, C. (2017) 'Boys outperform girls in 2017 computing A-levels.' *Computing Weekly*, 17 August. Accessed on 18/12/17 at www.computerweekly.com/news/450424647/Boys-outperform-girls-in-2017-computing-A-Levels.

Mettler, K. (2017) '"All of this grief": Prince Harry opens up about his mental health.' *The Washington Post*, 17 April. Accessed on 29/5/17 at www.washingtonpost.com/news/morning-mix/wp/2017/04/17/i-just-didnt-know-what-was-wrong-prince-harry-opens-up-about-his-mental-health/?utm_term=.084327a083c7.

Miracle, P. (2015) 'Understanding a mindset for success.' Accessed on 8/10/17 at http://gender.stanford.edu/news/2015/understanding-mindset-success.

Moffat, A. (2016) *No Outsiders in Our School*. London: Speechmark.

Mondschein, E.R., Adolph, K.E. and Tamis-LeMonda, C.S. (2000) 'Gender bias in mothers' expectations about infant crawling.' *Journal of Experimental Child Psychology 77*, 4, 304–316.

Moss, G. and Washbrook, L. (2016) *Understanding the Gender Gap in Literacy and Language Development*. Bristol: University of Bristol Graduate School of Education. Accessed on 12/5/17 at www.bristol.ac.uk/media-library/sites/education/documents/bristol-working-papers-in-education/Understanding%20the%20Gender%20Gap%20working%20paper.pdf.

Munsch, R. and Martchenko, M. (1980) *The Paper Bag Princess*. Toronto: Annick Press.

NASUWT (2017) 'Schools failing to protect teachers from online abuse.' Accessed on 18/4/17 at www.nasuwt.org.uk/article-listing/schools-failing-to-protect-teachers-online-abuse.html.

Ofsted (2011) 'Girls' Career Aspirations.' Accessed on 2/3/18 at www.gov.uk/government/publications/girls-career-aspirations.

Ofsted (2017) 'School inspection handbook for inspecting schools in England under section 5 of the Education Act 2005, October 2017, Ref no 150066.' Accessed on 1/12/17 at www.gov.uk/government/publications/school-inspection-handbook-from-september-2015.

OHCHR (Office of the United Nations High Commissioner for Human Rights) (1996–2017) *Convention on the Rights of the Child*. Accessed on 5/5/17 at www.ohchr.org/en/professionalinterest/pages/crc.aspx.

One Billion Rising (2017) '*Press release: V-Day's One Billion Rising is biggest global action ever to end violence against women and girls*.' Accessed on 13/5/17 at www.onebillionrising.org/394/press-release-v-days-one-billion-rising-is-biggest-global-action-ever-to-end-violence-against-women-and-girls.

ONS (Office for National Statistics) (2013) 'Focus on violent crime and sexual offenses 2011/12.' Accessed on 13/4/17 at http://webarchive.nationalarchives.gov.uk/20160105160709/http://www.ons.gov.uk/ons/dcp171778_298904.pdf.

Paechter, C.F. (2007) *Being Boys, Being Girls*. Maidenhead: Open University Press.

PISA (Programme for International Student Assessment) (2015) *The ABC of Gender Equality in Education: Aptitude, Behaviour, Confidence.* Paris: OECD Publishing. Accessed on 15/8/17 at www.oecd-ilibrary.org/education/the-abc-of-gender-equality-in-education_9789264229945-en.

Povey, H. (2017) *Engaging (with) Mathematics and Learning to Teach.* Münster: WTM.

PricewaterhouseCoopers LLP (2015) *The Costs of Eating Disorders. Social, Economic and Health Impacts.* Accessed on 21/4/16 at http://cdn.basw.co.uk/upload/basw_104500-2.pdf.

Renold, E. (2007) 'Primary school "studs" (de) constructing young boys' heterosexual masculinities.' *Men and Masculinities 9,* 3, 275–297.

Ringrose, J., Gill, R., Livingstone, S. and Harvey, L. (2012) *A Qualitative Study of Children, Young People and 'Sexting.'* Accessed on 29/5/17 at www.nspcc.org.uk/services-and-resources/research-and-resources/pre-2013/qualitative-study-sexting.

Safe Zone Project (n.d.) 'Core Vocabulary.' Accessed on 2/3/18 at http://thesafezoneproject.com/activity/core-vocabulary.

Samaritans (2016) 'Suicide Statistics Report 2016.' Accessed on 21/4/17 at www.samaritans.org/sites/default/files/kcfinder/files/Samaritans%20suicide%20statistics%20report%202016.pdf.

Sanday, P.R. (1981) 'The socio-cultural context of rape: A cross-cultural study.' *Journal of Social Issues 37,* 4, 5–27.

Siraj-Blatchford, I. and Clarke, P. (2000) *Supporting Identity, Diversity and Language in the Early Years.* Maidenhead: Open University Press.

Skelton, C. and Francis, B. (2003) *Boys and Girls in the Primary Classroom.* Maidenhead: Open University Press.

Skelton, C., Francis, B. and Valkanova, Y. (2007) *Breaking Down the Stereotypes: Gender and Achievement in Schools.* Equal Opportunities Commission. Accessed on 18/8/17 at https://core.ac.uk/download/pdf/4156138.pdf.

Slaughter, A. (2017) 'Imagine a world where gender is neither a plus nor a minus.' *National Geographic Magazine 'The Gender Revolution',* January. Accessed on 8/11/17 at www.nationalgeographic.com/magazine/2017/01/gender-future-anne-marie-slaughter.

Smith, C. (2014) *Gender and Participation in Mathematics and Further Mathematics A-levels: A Literature Review for the Further Mathematics Support Programme.* Institute of Education FMSP project. Accessed on 15/8/17 at http://furthermaths.org.uk/docs/Gender%20Literature%20Review%20FINAL%20Oct.pdf.

Steele, C.M. and Aronson, J. (1995) 'Stereotype threat and the intellectual test performance of African-Americans.' *Journal of Personality and Social Psychology 69,* 797–811.

Stroessner, S., Good, C. and Webster, L. (2014) *Reducing Stereotype Threat.* Accessed on 27/3/14 at www.reducingstereotypethreat.org/definition.html.

Szymanski, D.M., Moffitt, L.B. and Carr, E.R. (2011) 'Sexual objectification of women: Advances to theory and research.' *The Counseling Psychologist 39,* 1, 6–38.

Taafe, H. (2017) *Sounds Familiar.* Fawcett Society. Accessed on 13/4/17 at www.fawcettsociety.org.uk/Handlers/Download.ashx?IDMF=fbf75b5f-aee4-4624-8df4-833ffcc1a2d7.

TEDWomen (2010) *A Call to Men.* Accessed on 19/5/17 at www.ted.com/talks/tony_porter_a_call_to_men.

Thorne, B. (1993) *Gender Play: Girls and Boys in School.* Buckingham: Open University Press.

UNESCO (2017) 'Different meanings of "curriculum".' Accessed on 30/5/17 at www.unesco.org/new/en/education/themes/strengthening-education-systems/quality-framework/technical-notes/different-meaning-of-curriculum.

UN (United Nations) (2017) *Sustainable Development Goals.* Accessed on 18/12/17 at www.un.org/sustainabledevelopment/gender-equality.

University of Roehampton (2016) 'Better provision of computing needed in schools confirms new report.' Accessed on 17/8/17 at www.roehampton.ac.uk/news/2016/december/better-provision-of-computing-needed-in-schools-confirms-new-report.

UWE (University of the West of England) (2012) 'Beer belly is biggest body issue for men.' Accessed on 29/8/17 at https://info.uwe.ac.uk/news/uwenews/news.aspx?id=2178.

Upadyaya, K. and Eccles, J. (2014) 'Gender Differences in Teacher's Perceptions and Children's Ability Self Concepts.' In I. Schoon and J. Eccles (eds) *Gender Differences in Aspirations and Attainment: A Life Course Perspective.* Cambridge: Cambridge University Press.

Warrington, M., Younger, M. and McLellan, R. (2003) 'Under-achieving boys in English primary schools?' *The Curriculum Journal 14*, 2, 139–156.

Weigel, M. (2016) 'The long read: Political correctness: How the right invented a phantom enemy.' *The Guardian*, 30 November. Accessed on 9/2/18 at www.theguardian.com/us-news/2016/ nov/30/political-correctness-how-the-right-invented-phantom-enemy-donald-trump.

WHO (World Health Organization) (2013) 'Violence against women: The health sector responds.' Accessed on 13/5/17 at http://apps.who.int/iris/bitstream/10665/82753/1/WHO_NMH_ VIP_PVL_13.1_eng.pdf?ua=1.

Williams, M., Burden, R. and Lanvers, U. (2002) '"French is the language of love and stuff": Student perceptions of issues related to motivation in learning a foreign language.' *British Educational Research Journal 28*, 4, 503–527.

Wolpert, L. (2014) *Why Can't a Woman Be More Like a Man?* London: Faber & Faber.

Women's Aid Federation of England (2015) 'How common is domestic abuse?' Accessed on 13/4/17 at www.womensaid.org.uk/information-support/what-is-domestic-abuse/how-common-is-domestic-abuse.

Women's Sport and Fitness Foundation (2012) 'Changing the Game for Girls.' Accessed on 11/8/17 at www.sportdevelopment.org.uk/index.php/subjects/51-school/742-changing-the-game-for-girls.

World Economic Forum (2017) 'Global Gender Gap Report 2017.' Accessed on 2/3/18 at http:// reports.weforum.org/global-gender-gap-report-2017/global-gender-gap-index-2017.

Young Women's Trust (2016) 'Making apprenticeships work for young women.' Accessed on 2/3/18 at www.youngwomenstrust.org/apprenticeshipcampaign/making_apprenticeships_ work_for_young_women.

Zecharia, A., Cosgrave, E., Thomas, L. and Jones, R. (2014) 'Through both eyes: A case for a gender lens in STEM.' *Science Grrl.* Accessed on 15/8/17 at http://sciencegrrl.co.uk/assets/SCIENCE-GRRL-Stem-Report_FINAL_WEBLINKS-1.pdf.

Zosuls, K.M., Ruble, D.N., Tamis-LeMonda, C.S., Shrout, P.E., Bornstein, M.H. and Greulich, F.K. (2009) 'The acquisition of gender labels in infancy: Implications for sex-typed play.' *Developmental Psychology 45*, 3, 688–701.

Further Reading

Ball, R. and Millar, J. (2017) *The Gender Agenda: A First-Hand Account of How Girls and Boys Are Treated Differently.* London: Jessica Kingsley Publishers.

A fascinating day-by-day account of the different gender influences on a couple's son and daughter.

Bates, L. (2014) *Everyday Sexism...* London: Simon & Schuster.

The book of the, now international, website where Laura Bates captures girls and women's everyday experiences of sexism, sexual harassment and gender-based violence. A shocking but essential read which contextualises the very real need for work on gender equality in schools.

Fine, C. (2010) *Delusions of Gender: The Real Science Behind Sex Differences.* London: Icon Books.

Fine, C. (2017) *Testosterone Rex.* London: Icon Books.

Fine's books are fantastic antidotes to the popular brain-based theories about gender differences. Rigorously researched and beautifully written, these books document the neuroscientific evidence for the social construction of gender, describing how even hormones respond to environmental influences.

Lipman, M. (2003) *Thinking in Education.* Cambridge: Cambridge University Press.

For further reading about Philosophy for Children (P4C) from Lipman who, along with Ann Sharpe, developed this successful pedagogy now practised in more than 60 countries across the world.

Martin, B. (2011) *Children at Play: Learning Gender in the Early Years.* Stoke on Trent: Trentham Books Ltd.

In a detailed account of an interesting piece of participant research in a nursery setting in London, Martin gives an explanation of how young children learn to 'perform' their gender.

Paechter, C.F. (2007) *Being Boys, Being Girls.* Maidenhead: Open University Press.

This book brings together research on children and their construction and understanding of gender across the 0–18 age range with explicit suggestions for strategies and interventions.

Skelton, C. and Francis, B. (eds) (2003) *Boys and Girls in the Primary Classroom.* Maidenhead: Open University Press.

Each of the chapters in this book, written by an educator with expertise in a different area of the primary curriculum, summarises research and provides recommendations for practice.

Tayler, K. and Price, D. (2016) *Gender Diversity and Inclusion in Early Years Education.* Abingdon: Routledge.

A practical and accessible book for Early Years practitioners with chapters that cover a theoretical approach to gender development; current legislation and impact on Early Years practice; understanding gender fluidity and the way children express gender; creating gender equality when working with children, and the role of the manager in creating a supportive ethos.

Notes

PART 1

Chapter 1

1. All quotes from children are from DECSY 2016.
2. This book is based on the Development Education Centre South Yorkshire (DECSY)'s (www.decsy.org.uk) Gender Respect Project which brought together Early Years, primary and secondary teachers to develop curriculum materials and activities. These are available as a blog and as lesson plans at www.genderrespect2013.wordpress.com.
3. To give some examples: UK hospital admissions for eating disorders have increased in the last ten years. In 2015–2016, 91% were female, with the most common age groups being 10–14 and 15–19 (Health and Social Care Information Centre 2016, p.1).

   In 2015, a reported 725,000 people in the UK were suffering from eating disorders (PricewaterhouseCoopers LLP 2015).

   Men are three times as likely to commit suicide as women in the UK and 3.5 times as likely in the US (American Foundation for Suicide Prevention 2017; Samaritans 2016).

   > The rate of suicides in the UK increased in 2013, with the level among males its highest since 2001... Prof Louis Appleby, the chair of the National Suicide Prevention Advisory Group in England, said: 'Men are more at risk of suicide because they are more likely to drink heavily, use self-harm methods that are more often fatal and are reluctant to seek help.' (Davies 2015)

4. According to the Young Women's Trust, 'Women comprise 94% of childcare apprentices but just under 4% of engineering apprentices. Most strikingly, these figures have hardly changed in the last decade. In some cases they have even gone backwards. The percentage of female engineering apprentices has actually declined from 4.6% in 2002 to 3.8% in 2014' (2016, p.4).
5. The Fawcett Society states that 'The gender pay gap for women working full-time in Britain in 2017 is 14.1%' (2017a, p.1). One of the reasons for this was that 'Men tended to work in professional occupations associated with higher levels of pay. For example programmers and software development professionals earned £20.02 per hour (excluding overtime) while nurses earned on average £16.61 according to the 2012 Annual Survey of Hours and Earnings' (ONS 2013).
6. Only 32% of the seats held in the UK Parliament in 2017 were held by women (Apostolova and Cracknell 2017).

7. National Curriculum statutory assessments carried out in English primary schools at the end of KS1 and KS2 when most children are aged 7 and 11.

8. There has been a dramatic increase of referrals to the Gender Identity Development Service that work with children up to the age of 18 in the UK, rising from 50 in 2006 to over 1400 in 2016 (Presentation to Sheena Amos Youth Trust (SAYiT) 'Be a Part of Trans Forming Services' conference, 21 November 2016).

9. Private conversation (with permission) with Lee Lester, Sheena Amos Youth Trust (SAYiT), Sheffield, May 2017. SAYiT are receiving an increasing number of calls from schools asking support for transgender issues following Ofsted inspections.

10. It is estimated that one in three women in the world will experience physical and or sexual violence by a partner or sexual violence by a non-partner, hence the figure one billion, which is a third of all women (WHO 2013).

11. As defined by section 4 of the Equality Act 2010.

12. 'Goal 4: Ensure inclusive and equitable quality education and promote lifelong learning opportunities for all.

    4.5 By 2030, eliminate gender disparities in education.

    4.7 By 2030, ensure that all learners acquire the knowledge and skills needed to promote sustainable development, including, among others, through education for sustainable development and sustainable lifestyles, human rights, gender equality, promotion of a culture of peace and non-violence, global citizenship and appreciation of cultural diversity and of culture's contribution to sustainable development.

    4.a Build and upgrade education facilities that are child, disability and gender sensitive and provide safe, non-violent, inclusive and effective learning environments for all.

    Goal 5: Achieve gender equality and empower all women and girls.

    5.1 End all forms of discrimination against all women and girls everywhere.

    5.2 Eliminate all forms of violence against all women and girls in the public and private spheres, including trafficking and sexual and other types of exploitation.

    5.3 Eliminate all harmful practices, such as child, early and forced marriage and female genital mutilation.

    5.5 Ensure women's full and effective participation and equal opportunities for leadership at all levels of decision-making in political, economic and public life.

    5.c Adopt and strengthen sound policies and enforceable legislation for the promotion of gender equality and the empowerment of all women and girls at all levels.

    Goal 10: Reduce inequality within and among countries.

    10.2 By 2030, empower and promote the social, economic and political inclusion of all, irrespective of age, sex, disability, race, ethnicity, origin, religion or economic or other status' (UN 2017).

13. The plus sign is used with 'trans' to indicate a broader group of people who have identities that transgress socially defined gender norms.

Chapter 2

1. www.lettoysbetoys.org.uk.

2. www.pinkstinks.co.uk.

3. Studies have shown that even before their second birthday children are able to say to which sex they belong (Zosuls *et al.* 2009).

4. This girl had previously commented on a photograph of a female pilot saying, 'Girls are not used to flying planes and everything and sometimes they might not know

what they're doing and even if they've had training they might forget or something.' These comments might usefully have been followed up with a question which asked whether this is because they are women or whether men might forget as well, but at the time it seemed fairly apparent that this child meant that it was just women who would have this problem.

5.   www.reducingstereotypethreat.org.

Chapter 3

1.   According to Dweck, 'Fixed mindset – believing that your qualities are carved in stone'; 'growth mindset – (believing) that your basic qualities are things you can cultivate through efforts' (2006, pp.6, 7).

Chapter 4

1.   www.everydaysexism.com.
2.   For example, the PSHE Association, Brook and Sex Education Forum's 'Sex and Relationship Education (SRE) for the 21st century', available at www.pshe-association.org.uk/curriculum-and-resources.
3.   A policy and plan on SRE developed by one of the Gender Respect Project teachers for his primary school can be found at www.hindehouseprimary.net/Data/Parent_Downloads/SexandRelationshipEducation.pdf.

PART 2

Introduction

1.   Intersectionality: the theory that the overlap of different social identities such as gender, race, class and sexuality contribute to a specific type of discrimination experienced by an individual.
2.   An example of an 'Equality and Diversity' policy can be found at: www.pyebank.sheffield.sch.uk/virtual-office/policies.

Chapter 5

1.   Carol Dweck (2006) developed the idea of fixed and growth mindsets. A 'fixed mindset' is the belief that basic qualities like intelligence or talents are fixed traits. A 'growth mindset' is the belief that abilities can be developed through determination and hard work. 'Parents and teachers often offer well-meaning praise intended to bolster self-confidence that unfortunately can reinforce attributes of a fixed mindset rather than the process of effort, strategy, focus and perseverance that are essential to developing a growth mindset. Phrases like, "You're so smart! You got an A without even studying," or "You won that race so easily, you're going to be an Olympic athlete!" may be intended to show support and boost self-esteem, but the hidden messages convey quite the opposite: "If I don't learn easily, I'm not smart." "I shouldn't try doing anything hard, or I might be a failure"' (Miracle 2015).
2.   www.implicit.harvard.edu/implicit/iatdetails.html.
3.   The use of 'guys' is quite common but has its own problems as it is a word which means men and so makes women and girls invisible. The equivalent word for women, 'gals', wouldn't be seen as an appropriate term for a mixed group of men and women (see Jascz 2015).

4.   See www.readingrockets.org/strategies/reciprocal_teaching.
5.   A Google image search in August 2017 for 'prom' revealed pages and pages of images of male/female couples with the girls/women wearing sparkly long dresses and the men in suits.

Chapter 6

1.   The subjects named are those that are in the English National Curriculum 2014; see www.gov.uk/government/uploads/system/uploads/attachment_data/file/425601/PRIMARY_national_curriculum.pdf.
2.   www.biographyonline.net/people/world-peace.html.
3.   In 2017, GCSE French, 18.8% of boys and 26.6% of girls achieved grade A/7 with 63.5% of boys and 73.7% of girls achieving grade C/4. In 2017, GCSE German 20% of boys and 26.7% of girls achieved grade A/7 and 70% of boys and 79% of girls achieved grade C/4. Only 2917 boys compared to 6551 girls sat A level French in 2017 and 1554 boys compared to 2109 girls sat A level German in 2017 (Joint Council for Qualifications 2017).
4.   Research has found that some boys see French as a girls' subject. See, for example, Williams, Burden and Lanvers (2002).
5.   https://genderstats.un.org/#/home.
6.   http://mathsci2.appstate.edu/~sjg/ncctm/activities/hypatia/hypatia.pdf.
7.   http://mathsci2.appstate.edu/~sjg/ncctm/activities/Florence3.pdf.

Chapter 7

1.   My explanation of P4C is adapted from my chapter (Griffin 2014) on P4C in *Developing Global Schools in China: East Meets West.*
2.   Society for the Advancement of Philosophy Enquiry and Reflection in Education (www.sapere.org.uk), the body that promotes P4C throughout the UK. IAPC (Institute for the Advancement of Philosophy for Children), based at Montclair University, where Lipman and Sharpe developed P4C, provides training in the USA.
3.   P4C Level 1 is a two-day course to introduce P4C and enable teachers to start practising with their students. Level 2a and Level 2b, four days in total, advance P4C skills and develop school leadership in P4C.
4.   Available from various UNICEF websites including Rights Respecting Schools in Canada, https://rrscanada.files.wordpress.com/2013/09/rights-wants-and-needs-activity-kit.pdf.
5.   There is also a book of the film, *The Green Bicycle* by Haifaa al-Mansour (2016).
6.   Tables contain parliamentary information licensed under the Open Parliament License v3.0.
7.   www.bbc.co.uk/newsround/29443373.
8.   www.youtube.com/watch?v=G7l6crlMOrw.
9.   www.futuremorph.org/wp-content/uploads/games/interactive/index.html.
10. National Careers Service, Job Profiles, https://nationalcareersservice.direct.gov.uk/job-profiles/home.
11. https://nationalcareersservice.direct.gov.uk/get-a-job.
12. With these and any materials which are about potentially sensitive topics, please watch the films carefully in advance to check their suitability for your particular group of students and make sure you have support in place for any individual students who might find the issue difficult.

13. www.sliptalk.com/normal-wedding-photo.
14. www.sliptalk.com/normal-wedding-photo.
15. www.youtube.com/watch?v=iYhCn0jf46U.
16. Adapted, with permission, from Lyle, S. (2014) 'Violence and prejudice: Giving young people the skills to think independently.' *Creative Teaching & Learning 5.1*, 62–67. Later published on the Gender Respect website, https:genderrespect2013. wordpress.com/2014/09/22/violence-and-prejudice-activites.
17. 'Do it yourself' – used in the UK to include mending and making jobs in the home involving building, decorating, carpentry, plumbing and electrics without employing professionals.
18. The films of both conferences are available at https://genderrespect2013.wordpress. com.
19. The PowerPoint presentation, poetry workshop and senses sheet are all available on the Gender Respect website at www.genderrespect2013.wordpress.com/teaching-ideas/one-billion-rising.
20. www.onebillionrising.org/about/campaign/one-billion-rising.
21. www.genderrespect2013.wordpress.com/teaching-ideas/one-billion-rising.

Appendix 4

1. www.amightygirl.com/books?p=73.
2. www.letterboxlibrary.com.

Index